Thinking in
PostScript

Thinking in
PostScript®

Glenn C. Reid

Addison-Wesley Publishing Company, Inc.

Reading, Massachusetts • Menlo Park, California • New York
Don Mills, Ontario • Wokingham, England • Amsterdam • Bonn
Sydney • Singapore • Tokyo • Madrid • San Juan

Library of Congress Cataloging-in-Publication Data

Reid, Glenn C.

       Thinking in PostScript / Glenn C. Reid.

          p.   cm.

       Includes indexes.

       ISBN 0-201-52372-8

       1. PostScript (Computer program language)   I. Title.

QA76.73.P67R46   1990

005.26'2—dc20   90-43721

                                                         CIP

Many of the designations used by manufacturers and sellers to distinguish their products are claimed as trademarks. Where those designations appear in this book and Addison-Wesley was aware of a trademark claim, the designations have been printed in initial capital letters.

The name *PostScript*® is a registered trademark of Adobe Systems Incorporated (Adobe). All instances of the name *PostScript* in the text are references to the PostScript language as defined by Adobe unless otherwise stated. The name *PostScript* also is used as a product trademark for Adobe's implementation of the PostScript language interpreter.

Any references to a PostScript printer, a PostScript file, or a PostScript driver refer to printers, files, and driver programs (respectively) that are written in or that support the PostScript language.

Sponsoring Editor: Carole McClendon
Technical Reviewer: Ken Anderson
Cover Design: Doliber Skeffington
Text Design: Rex Holmes
Set in 10-Point Times Roman

ABCDEFGHIJ-MW-943210
First printing, September, 1990

Table of Contents

Preface

This book is intended to provide a practical, intriguing, and fresh look at the PostScript programming language. PostScript is a mysterious language, powerful and cryptic. It is expressive and complicated and yet surprisingly simple. In order to master a programming language, you have to learn to think like the compiler or interpreter, and instinctively know how to solve problems. You develop a "tool kit" of useful approaches, proven solutions, and techniques. You reach an understanding that is based on analogy and connections with other things that you know.

This book helps you build a solid foundation of understanding for the PostScript language. It teaches you to become an expert programmer and to have confidence that you have written the best possible PostScript program. It shows you how to combine the elements of the language into a strong, well-designed, modular program that is easy to develop and maintain. It is not a problem-solving book, nor simply a reference to the language; it is a guide to developing programming techniques and to learning how to use the PostScript tool kit, which is filled with hundreds of individual operators.

Comparisons are drawn to other programming languages throughout the book, particularly to C, which is a very common language and one that is often used in the same environments where the PostScript language is found. If you are a competent C or Pascal programmer but you have had limited exposure to PostScript, this book should be exactly what you need. If you are a BASIC, Forth, or Lisp programmer, you should find this book at just the right level for introducing you to the PostScript language.

If you think of yourself as an expert PostScript programmer, you will still find some useful techniques in this book, and it is a very worthwhile addition to your library of PostScript books, since it overlaps very little with existing material.

The most fundamental level of a program is the set of techniques used in the development of the program itself, regardless of what the program does. This book addresses that area of PostScript programming in a way rooted partly in computer science theory, encompassing algorithms and data structures, but it is very practically oriented toward real-world programming and programmers.

Each chapter contains a section of Exercises. You should find these problems easy to solve if you have understood the concepts in the chapter. Many concepts do not gel fully without some direct application to a problem. In these cases, the exercises should stimulate you to think about the issues that have been presented and give you a chance to confront a situation that requires you to apply your knowledge. The appendix contains answers to the exercises.

To give you a feel for what this book is about and to whet your appetite, the following code segment illustrates a common (though advanced) technique that is used in many PostScript programs. If you instantly recognize what it does and could have written it yourself, then you may use this book to discover other techniques that you may not have yet encountered. If this example seems mysterious or you have to spend a lot of time analyzing it, then you need this book to help you start thinking this way.

```
% print out all the elements in an array or procedure
dup type /arraytype eq 1 index type /packedarraytype eq or { %ifelse
        0 exch { %forall
                exch dup (XXX) cvs print (: ) print 1 add exch ==
        } forall pop
}{ pop } ifelse
```

This particular example is a bit advanced and special-purpose, but it should not be intimidating even to a beginning or intermediate programmer. A typical question in an end-of-chapter exercise might be "Rewrite the previous program fragment using local variables rather than using the operand stack."

In order to get the maximum benefit from this book, you probably should have written at least one program—from scratch—longer than 100 lines of code (and gotten it to work correctly). This program might have been written in virtually any programming language. If you then modified the program for an additional 100 hours after it first started to work, if you understand variables, arrays, and strings—and if you want to become a very good PostScript programmer—then you are an ideal candidate for this book.

Chapter 1

PostScript as a
Programming Language

It probably is true that PostScript is not everyone's first choice as a programming language. But let's put that premise behind us, and assume that you need (or want) to write a program in the PostScript language. How do you become an expert in this language, and how do you develop the instincts and learn the techniques necessary to tackle challenging problems with confidence?

As a programming language, PostScript is somewhat unusual—and frankly, many of the programming instincts you've developed from using other languages may not be directly applicable with the PostScript language. The first few chapters of this book help you put PostScript into perspective by comparing it to languages you probably already know, such as C. There are stronger similarities between PostScript and, say, Forth or Lisp, but if you are expert in either of those languages you probably won't have much trouble mastering PostScript.

Every programming language was designed with a specific purpose, even if that purpose was to be a "general-purpose programming language." To use a language effectively, you should understand its design and learn its strengths and weaknesses. PostScript is a full-fledged programming language, and it is possible to accomplish almost any task with it. It includes many high-level language constructs and data structures. The PostScript language is a tool kit filled with hundreds of special-purpose tools. Mastery of the language teaches you to select just the right instrument, swiftly and instinctively, and to use it effectively.

DESIGN FEATURES

PostScript's most obvious language features are that it is an interpreted language, it is stack-based, and it is heavily oriented toward graphics and typography. These design choices were all made in order to make it useful as a device-independent page description language for imaging on raster devices. These language features also make it a fairly unusual language in which to write programs.

The PostScript language is stack-based (resulting in "backwards" syntax) primarily so that a program can be evaluated with very low overhead in processing and storage. Each instruction can be acted upon immediately, without the need to buffer large amounts of the program.

PostScript is interpreted (rather than compiled) for a couple of reasons. The most obvious one is device independence. If the program remains in source form until it reaches its final destination, it is extremely portable to new computer environments, processors, etc. It is an interpreted language also because documents are often transmitted long distances, archived, or saved and printed many times, and this enables the documents to remain in ASCII text source form for better life expectancy and resiliency in a device-independent environment.

And finally, PostScript is heavily biased toward graphic imaging and typography because it was originally conceived as a mechanism to control raster imaging devices like laser printers and display screens.

The design choices made in the PostScript language have quite an impact on the programmer's experiences in mastering the language, but they were not made arbitrarily, nor intended to make the programmer's life more difficult.

STRUCTURED PROGRAMMING TECHNIQUES

If you have had any formal training in programming, you are familiar with the various structured programming techniques, up through and including object-oriented programming. These techniques vary, but are largely based on the concept of a procedure, or a modular functional unit (sometimes called a *black box*). A black box is typically any set of operations that has a specific input and output and performs a single task. The mechanics of the operation are hidden from one who uses the black box. This is the notion behind writing procedures, creating software libraries, object-oriented programming, block-structured code; it is a widely recognized technique in computer science.

To start out, PostScript simply isn't well suited to structured programming, and if you try too hard to formalize the interfaces, declare local variables, and observe many tried and true programming practices, you may end up with a complicated, inefficient, and ill-designed program. On the other hand, if you ignore structured programming techniques and write code off the top of your head, you will probably have something worse. The trick is to borrow enough of the useful concepts from structured programming to make programs readable, easy to maintain, easily debugged, and efficient, while using the expressive power of the language to your advantage.

There is no concept of **goto** in the PostScript language, or even explicit control transfer, so you don't have to worry about that particular dogmatic concern. You do have to be careful about procedure-calling interfaces, where they exist, since all program checking is done at run-time.

Many of the concepts in structured programming can be used quite effectively in PostScript. You can define procedures to help you share similar code across parts of your program. You can use the operand stack for your temporary data rather than having many global variables. You can design interfaces between components of your program and pass parametric information on the stack. You can even define functions that return results onto the stack for use by other procedures.

PROGRAMMING TASKS

There are many different kinds of tasks associated with programming. There are data-crunching tasks, user interface tasks, communication with other computers or programs, file operations, graphics, and various others. In some tasks, such as numerical computation, the algorithm by which the task is carried out is of the utmost importance, both for accuracy and for performance. Other tasks, such as user interfaces and graphics, are much more results oriented: what is important is whether it looks good and/or works well. In file operations, arguably the accuracy with which the operations are carried out is the most important aspect of the task, and the algorithm and performance of the task are secondary.

The nature of the task has a strong influence on the programming style and technique. If your purpose is to draw graphics, your programming efforts should be minimal, clear, and used only to streamline the process of drawing. In the PostScript language in particular, graphics programming is the means to the end, not the end in itself. The *PostScript Language Reference Manual* mentions that any marks made on the page are a side effect of the execution of the program, but from your perspective as a programmer, it is the other way around. The fact that you have to write PostScript programs is a side effect of the fact that you are trying to draw pictures on a PostScript-based system.

WINDOW SYSTEMS, COMMUNICATIONS, AND DISPLAYS

Recently, the PostScript language has evolved from a printer control language into a communications medium on host computers. There are window systems and networks based on the PostScript language. In light of this, there are many new kinds of programming tasks that must be (or can be) carried out in the PostScript language.

One of the more interesting aspects of a window system or communications environment based on a programming language is that you can send an algorithmic description of the picture you want drawn (or of the operation you want carried out) instead of the individual bits or instructions. For instance, if you wanted to draw a grid of parallel lines, both horizontally and vertically, you might express this graphic operation (which has a strongly repetitive basis) as two loops of instructions. (See Example 1.1. The results of Example 1.1 are shown in Figure 1.1).

Example 1.1: Repetitive Algorithms

```
% 18-pt spacing, 24 lines
0 18 18 24 mul { %for
        dup 0 moveto
        600 lineto
} for stroke

% 18-pt spacing, 36 lines
0 18 18 36 mul { %for
        dup 0 exch moveto
        436 exch lineto
} for stroke
```

Figure 1.1: Output of Example 1.1

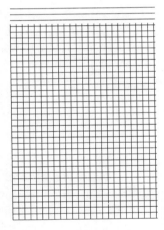

This is quite a bit more compact than it would be to draw 60 individual lines, each with its own coordinates and **moveto** and **lineto** instructions. In this particular example, 25 percent of the data end up being **0**; just avoiding the transmission of those zeroes is significant. The loops above consist of 30 PostScript language tokens to be transmitted, whereas the same program done with **moveto** and **lineto** instructions would require 360 PostScript tokens.

In addition to providing power and compactness of representation, having an interpreted programming language at the network and graphics layer of a computer system provides a very neat solution to problems of transportability and machine independence, since many of the decisions are delayed until run-time. One important concept in object-oriented programming in general is to keep the interface between objects clean enough that there are not any problems when you hook them together. This is especially important where you have to write programs at the places where objects meet. It is important for you, the reader and programmer, to understand PostScript well enough to create programs that behave well in the nested, shared, cut-and-pasted environments that exist today.

DATA STRUCTURES AND ALGORITHMS

The classic view of a computer program is a synthesis of data structures and algorithms. Books often have titles that contain these two words, and every program probably has one or the other in it somewhere. If you use PostScript to describe pages and to drive laser printers, your need for real data storage and computation should be minimal. However, if you use PostScript in a windowing environment to arbitrate input events from the keyboard (as an extreme example), you will definitely need to create data structures and implement some potentially difficult algorithms.

CONCLUDING THOUGHTS

The next several chapters help you build some solid approaches to PostScript data structures and help you master the language elements thoroughly so that you will feel comfortable implementing your favorite algorithms. In particular, the data types unique to PostScript are explored (dictionaries and names) as well as traditional data types such as strings, arrays, and numbers. Other chapters are devoted entirely to seemingly simple things like the **ifelse** operator or looping. However, since PostScript was not originally designed for heavy programming, these traditional programming techniques have never been thoroughly addressed. And you simply can't write a serious PostScript program without using **ifelse** or writing a procedure or two.

EXERCISES

Each chapter in this book comes with some exercises at the end of it, to help you to test your understanding of the concepts presented. Since this first chapter has taken a philosophical overview of PostScript as a programming language, the exercises are more like essay questions than problems.

1. Why do you want to write a PostScript program? (This is a serious question, and one which should be given some thought; reflection on *why* may provide you with good horse sense throughout your programming experience.)

2. Why is PostScript a "backwards" language, in which the operators come *after* the operands?

3. Why is PostScript an interpreted language?

4. Why is it silly to write fractal programs in PostScript?

Chapter 2

PostScript is Not Like C

Many programmers try to treat a new language as if it were an old language with which they are already familiar. "If you know one programming language, you know them all." That is somewhat true with procedural languages like C, Pascal, Modula 3, or maybe FORTRAN. There are only so many ways to say **if** ... **then** ... **else**, and once you learn one language, you can learn the others without too much difficulty. These languages typically only have a dozen or so language elements; if you were to name all the "reserved words" in Pascal or C, how many would you come up with? If you named the built-in features of the language, you wouldn't get much past control structures, procedure definitions, data types, and input/output capabilities. These languages are general-purpose procedural languages.

But PostScript has over 300 individual special-purpose operators, it is interpreted rather than compiled, it uses post-fix notation, and is quite different from C. This is good, to a large extent, but again, you need to understand the differences rather than to take the posture that it's just another language.

In a procedural language, the interface between components of a program is formalized in the notion of a procedure call. (For more information about procedures, see Chapter 9). The program is typically written as a series of modular procedures or functions, with a well-defined calling mechanism for transferring control and passing data between the modules. This calling mechanism is artificial, and is apparent only at the programming language level. When compiled, the data (or pointers to the data) are in fact placed on the operand stack of the hardware processor, and an instruction to jump to a subroutine (JSR) is issued to transfer control to the other procedure, which then uses the data on the stack. The notion of type checking is carried out at the language level by requiring that the data be declared to be of an explicit type as the data are being passed to or from a procedure or function.

When writing C programs, the programmer designs the modules, the interfaces, and the interaction between them. The data structures are designed to work cleanly within the modular design of the program, and the parameters to the various procedures are set up to pass data appropriately between the modules or procedures. Data types and structures should be appropriate for the task at hand; some of them are made *globally* visible (and therefore can be used throughout the entire program); others are *local* to a particular procedure (and can be used only within that procedure). A fairly high percentage of coding time is spent just selecting names for data types, structure elements, procedures, variables, and modules. The names given to these program elements contribute heavily to the readability and maintainability of the code.

The PostScript language is an interesting hybrid between high-level and low-level languages. It is high level in the sense that there are individual operators that encompass very powerful functionality (the **show** operator, for example), yet the mechanics of the language are less structured than other high-level languages, and the manipulation of objects on the operand stack more closely resembles assembly-language programming.

COMPARISON OF LANGUAGE MECHANISMS

One of the first skills a programmer develops is the ability to conceptualize the procedures that will be needed for a program to be implemented effectively. These procedures are designed by deciding what data are needed, how that data ought to be passed through the control sequence of the program, and how the naming of the procedures will contribute to the readability and flow of the program. Procedures should not be too big and complex, nor too small and inefficient.

There is a major difference between PostScript and C that makes program design completely different. In C, you basically have no built-in language elements. There are a few control structures, loop constructs, some input/output operations, and the inherent procedure call mechanism, but there aren't a lot of individual operators as there are in PostScript. In a sense, the entire program design is based on the implementation of procedures or modules.

In PostScript program design, almost the opposite is true. There are well over 300 individual PostScript operators. Very efficient, well-designed programs can be constructed without ever writing a single procedure, just by using the built-in operators. Then, when the functionality of the program fully emerges, the ability to define procedures can help you to organize the code or to make it more efficient, but usually it is not a good approach to begin by designing the procedures themselves, since the work is ultimately carried out by the individual operators anyway.

TIP

A PostScript procedure is simply a set of operations that are grouped together and that can be invoked by a single instruction. They do not replace the individual operations, they merely provide another way to cause them to be executed. The principle advantages to defining procedures is to collect sequences of operations that may be performed repeatedly.

Furthermore, the operand stack is the communication area between procedures; it is the only place where you can pass data between procedures. But, since this is also the way data are passed to individual PostScript operators, the distinction between a sequence of PostScript operators in-line versus grouped into a procedure is not particularly great. The differences amount to the ordering of operands and whether data are interleaved with instructions or pushed as a series of operands before the procedure is invoked. This difference is crucial only for readability, organization, and efficiency, and it is never required to define a procedure for good program flow.

EXPRESSING AN ALGORITHM AS A PROGRAM

If you start with a flowchart to represent an algorithm, the components of the flowchart are somewhat abstract. They represent actions and objects that are traditionally found in programming languages, and the structure and control flow of the program are represented symbolically. The use of a flowchart is predicated on the notion that the program's algorithm can be embodied in a diagram showing the steps required to carry out the task.

Each program's implementation is affected strongly by the language itself. Design decisions must be made based on the inherent strengths and weaknesses of the language, and the details of the implementation must ultimately be expressed using the native language constructs.

In order to represent your flowcharted algorithm as a program in some programming language, you must apply the language elements appropriately, within a structure you design. To do this, the language you are using must be fully general and must allow conditional expressions and be able to transfer control to other parts of the program. Yet each programming language was created with a particular purpose in mind, and each programming task is bent and shaped by the language in which it is implemented. The language provides the foundation. Beyond that, it is your skill as a programmer that creates a working program from the building blocks of the language. This is the art of programming.

Although it is possible to start with an abstract algorithm and then implement it in whatever programming language is handy, it is probably more realistic to assume that algorithms are developed in light of a particular language, and in such a way as to take advantage of that language's features. For example, the kinds of data structures that exist (or are easy to implement) in a language can greatly affect the approach to solving the programming problem. PostScript has a specialized dictionary data structure that can provide entirely new approaches to problems where one might end up implementing lots of pointers and structures in a C program.

THE UNIX SHELL AND OPERATING SYSTEM

There are some interesting similarities between the PostScript language and the command-line interface to the UNIX operating system. At first glance, they are quite dissimilar; one is a programming language, the other is an operating system. But consider that the shell program at which the user types UNIX commands is in fact an interpreter. The shell supports a very simple programming framework, with loops and conditionals, and has a few real operators built in. It is intended only as a skeletal environment, and the UNIX programs themselves provide most of the language elements for shell programs.

The PostScript language has an extensible set of operators, each of which is invoked by name (for example, **moveto**). The names are looked up, at run-time, in the dictionary stack of the interpreter. This is exactly analogous to the UNIX shell, which has an extensible command set and a name lookup mechanism through which all commands are invoked. The name lookup is controlled by the concept of a *search path*, or an ordered set of directories in which to look for the named program. Either language can be extended simply by adding another name into the search path, and using it in the same way that the existing names are used.

TIP

Here's a trick that you may find very helpful in assimilating the large space of operators in the PostScript language. (It evolved from my mechanism for learning about UNIX.) If you are having a difficult time with a particular part of your program or you think to yourself that there must be a better way, the chances are that the designers of the language encountered the same situation, and designed an operator that exactly solves the problem. Quickly review a summary list of operators (see the Appendix) to see if there is some other operator that could make short work of your task.

Furthermore, both the PostScript language and the UNIX operating system offer a very large and relatively flat set of operators or commands, making the basic language easy to learn, but offering a very rich and sometimes intimidating array of possibilities.

Data are not shared in the same way in the UNIX shell as they are in the PostScript language, since the shell provides a pipeline mechanism for communicating between processes, whereas the PostScript language has an operand stack where all operators look for their operands (and leave their results).

The comparison with the UNIX operating system is offered only to trick you into thinking about the language as a set of powerful operators set in the framework of a simple interpreted programming language. If you are an experienced UNIX programmer, you probably have developed a feel for the kinds of problems that are best solved with shell scripts versus those that require the writing of full-fledged C programs. If your PostScript programming task is in an environment where you have the opportunity to balance the work load between a C program and a PostScript program (in a client/server environment for example), this analogy may give you a feel for the kinds of tasks that might be more appropriate for each side of the equation.

INPUT, OUTPUT, AND THROUGHPUT

A program is usually only as good as the data you put through it. Most programs do not come with data already in them, you have to provide the data, and wait for the program to provide output based on the input. This is also true with PostScript, although the input and output may depend on the environment in which the program operates. For example, a PostScript program is often just a vehicle for printing or displaying information. In this sense, the data are provided *en masse* from a document, and the output of the program is simply the display or printing of the data in the document.

The input and output of a program depend greatly upon the environment in which the program is running. If your PostScript program is running on an interpreter built into your laser printer, there are few choices for input and output. The input can either come from the cable leading into the laser printer (which is also where the program comes from, typically) or it can come from an internal disk system built into the printer. The choices of output are the same, although the output can also be the printed page itself (which is normally the whole point of PostScript programming). In this case, the throughput of the program can be measured by how fast the pages print when you send it your program to draw pictures. And it is very much up to you and your program to control how fast those pages print.

The vast majority of all computer programs in existence today simply read data from a file, let you edit the data in some way, and then write it back to a file again. These are thought of as editors, word processors, spread sheets, drawing programs, statistical packages, and so forth. The files they read and write are documents. For the most part, documents are not interchangeable between systems or programs, so you just read into and write out from your single program, and hope to glean something useful from the data itself when the document is visible in the program.

PostScript programs rarely operate directly on files and usually are not constructed just to rearrange bodies of data. PostScript is a language designed for expression of visual images, communication of data to remote systems, and one-way data manipulation. Throughput is everything. PostScript programs are perhaps more analogous to utility programs or device drivers, where the task is not to perform a specific application task, but to provide a general mechanism for accomplishing data transfer, imaging, or device control. The input may well be arbitrary (as opposed to a carefully constructed data file), and the output may be simply a sheet of paper with some marks on the surface.

CONCLUDING THOUGHTS

This chapter positions PostScript alongside popular conventional languages such as C, to point out the similarities and differences in a slightly abstract sense. The ideas presented may raise more questions than they provide answers, but they should arm you with a sense of perspective on the PostScript language that will help you approach challenging programming tasks with some imagination, confidence, and with open eyes. The comparison with C, in particular, might help by convincing you to revisit some old habits of programming as you implement the guts of your program. Writing loops, making simple **ifelse** statements, and inventing variables should be done with a full appreciation of the language and understanding of its strengths and weaknesses.

The next chapters get increasingly specific about the PostScript language and help you to build a solid foundation of programming skills.

EXERCISES

1. Rewrite the following C program segment in PostScript:

    ```
    factorial = 1;
    for ( index = 10; index > 0; index-- )
    {
        factorial = factorial * index;
    }
    printf ( "10 factorial is %d\n", factorial );
    ```

2. What would you say are PostScript's greatest strengths as a general-purpose programming language? What are its greatest weakness?

3. Name four basic language constructs that are available in both the C and PostScript languages (or, if you don't know C, pick any language of your choice).

4. Name three things provided in the PostScript language that are not provided as a standard part of any other language.

Chapter 3

Foundations

This chapter presents some fundamental concepts for programming in PostScript. Some of the information may seem extremely introductory and perhaps carried over from other languages, but there are many tips and techniques presented that should benefit even the seasoned PostScript programmer.

The chapter starts with a basic paradigm of program development that will serve as a foundation for developing PostScript programming skills. This paradigm is certainly not the best or the only approach to constructing programs, but it may help even to contrast the steps with your own thoughts on software development.

There is a cyclic pattern to all kinds of program development, although it varies considerably based on the tools and the environment in which you are working. To build the PostScript programming paradigm, we will look at the sequence of steps involved in learning to develop software in a new language or on an unfamiliar system (see Example 3.1). The list may seem a little light-hearted in places, but is an attempt to accurately identify the learning curve and problem areas that real people encounter.

Example 3.1: The Programming Cycle

1. Get a trivial "Hello world" example program working, proving to yourself that the basic system is working correctly, your documentation isn't lying to you, and that it is possible to construct a working program in your environment.

2. Excitedly type in a one-page program that you designed on a legal pad, and attempt to get it to work. At this stage it is difficult to tell why your program isn't working, because it typically just doesn't do anything, so you have nowhere to start in debugging it.

3. Find some simple oversight that caused your program not to work, like the lack of a **begin** or a **%!** or something trivial.

4. Develop a skeleton program, either in your mind or in a file, that has all of the basic ingredients necessary for a working program, based on the lessons learned in Steps 1, 2, and 3.

5. Develop several small, useful, working programs using some of the basic language constructs you have learned.

6. Attempt to tackle something bigger, or a new language construct, but with a solid foundation on which to test and debug.

7. Get confused by the documentation for new language features, causing the program to become buggy. Learn some ad-hoc debugging skills based on your frustration in finding the bugs in your program.

8. Go back and read the introduction to your documentation and learn that your basic model of the programming language was slightly incorrect. Adjust your thinking accordingly.

9. Create an entirely new skeletal program and get it to work.

10. Be inspired by your new, working program and begin to think of features to add.

11. Develop a rough working feature, inventing procedures, variables, and interfaces as you go.

12. Attempt to fit the new feature into the skeleton of your working program; readjust the basic framework slightly to accommodate it.

13. Test the new feature, and discover some bugs, some related to the basic workings of the original program.

---

14. Debug the new feature thoroughly, getting it to work well with the existing program.

15. Go back to Step 10 and repeat through Step 15 indefinitely

Steps 1 through 9 in this list represent the learning curve for a new language or system, before you have become comfortable with the process. Steps 10 through 15 comprise one view of the basic software cycle for a single-person programming project (without a lot of advance planning, which is typical of most programming projects).

The software cycle is very important to consider because it very much affects the quality of the programs you write. You may adopt techniques during your learning phase that lead to very poor quality programs, but you may not even know it. You may introduce fundamentally bad design or deeply-rooted bugs during the development process that could have been prevented had you designed the entire program at the beginning, or if your techniques had been sound enough to prevent cancer in the core of your software.

Good programming skills will make your PostScript programming task much more successful and enjoyable. Some of the techniques presented in this and subsequent chapters should strike a chord with you and help you to develop a sound methodology of your own.

POSTSCRIPT LANGUAGE SYNTAX

One of the first problems that beginning programmers encounter when learning a new language is how to get the basic syntax right. It seems trivial once you get past it, but the first step always is learning how to represent strings, how to divide two numbers, how to find mismatched brackets, or any of the other details involved in getting a simple program to work.

In order to write good, solid programs, it is important to understand the syntax of the language well enough that you can write legal, working code instinctively, without hesitating about whether you need a slash, a backslash, parentheses, or curly braces. Luckily, the rules for PostScript syntax are pretty straightforward and easily remembered. Rather than providing an exhaustive review of the language syntax and representation, the following section presents some "seat of the pants" rules that should be all you need to avoid syntactic problems when you are writing PostScript programs.

Here are some general rules of thumb to help you with PostScript language syntax. These rules should help you avoid common pitfalls.

- Make sure all your delimiters match; for instance, { }, ( ), and [ ]. Using good indentation style will help you avoid the problems of mismatched or missing delimiters.
- Use parentheses for string delimiters (rather than quotation marks, as used in other languages). If your string contains parentheses or backslashes, quote them with a backslash, as in the following string:
  (this string contains two parens \) and \(a backslash \\ )
- Always use a slash that leans to the right for literal names, as in **/Palatino-Roman** or **/MyEncoding**. There is nothing special about the slash, it just keeps the name from getting executed immediately. Instead, it lets the name be put on the operand stack.
- Remember that the operators always come after the operands (postfix notation). The order of the operands on the stack makes the rightmost operand the one at the top of the stack (closest to the operator itself).
- Spaces, tabs, and newlines are all treated as white space. Use them wisely to make your program layout more readable.
- Anything following a % (through the end of the line) is treated as a comment, unless the % is inside a string body (in parentheses).

In practice, you will probably not encounter very many syntax errors. It is much more likely that the execution of your program will go astray with a **typecheck** or **stackunderflow** error, indicating that you gave the wrong arguments to some operator. If you can look at the contents of the operand stack when the error occurs, you will usually be able to find the problem quickly.

SIMPLE PROGRAM STRUCTURE

There is no enforced structure to a PostScript program. You don't need to start the program with a magic word like **Begin**, nor end it with anything special. You don't have to declare variables at the beginning of the file, you don't have to declare procedures in any particular order. The only checking is done when you run the program. If it works, it works. If it doesn't, you will get an error message explaining why it doesn't work.

However, since most people who read your program (including you, most likely) are used to seeing some structure in code, there is a strong case for structuring your program carefully. If nothing else, it will help you to maintain the program, to update it and revise it as necessary.

Make Definitions First

Typically, a PostScript program contains a fair number of definitions, either procedure definitions or variables of some kind. In general, you should define these up front in the PostScript program. A good approach is to set up all the named objects you will need at the beginning of the program, then set up all the procedures, then begin to call them by name at the appropriate time. This is in fact very similar to the traditional structure found in other programming languages, where the definitions must come before the procedures. Example 3.2 shows some definitions of objects that can then be referenced by name later in the program.

Example 3.2: Defining and Using Named Objects

```
% an often-used font stored as a named object
/headerfont /Times-Bold findfont 24 scalefont def

% using the named font object
headerfont setfont
72 600 moveto
(Section 1.1) show
```

For PostScript page descriptions (documents), Adobe Systems has defined *PostScript Document Structuring Conventions* that break a document file down into several components. The first component, the *prologue*, consists only of definitions that may be referenced by the rest of the document. The rest of the document is composed of *pages*, with an optional *setup* section before the pages. These structuring conventions make it easier for post-processing programs such as print spoolers to manipulate the files in helpful ways.

In a PostScript program that is not a page description, these delineations don't make quite as much sense, but it is still helpful to make the definitions at the beginning of the program. An exception to this rule is that if a procedure requires some data structures for its operation but they must be defined outside the procedure, it is often best to group them with the procedure, to make the program easier to maintain (see Example 3.3).

Example 3.3: Keeping Variables with Procedure Definitions

```
/filebuff 1024 string def
/countlines { %def
        0                   % counter on stack
        /fd (filename) (r) file def
        { %loop
                fd filebuff readline { %ifelse
                        pop 1 add
                }{ %else
                        pop 1 add exit
                } ifelse
        } loop
} bind def

/specialchar (\037) def
/parsestring { %def
        specialchar search {
                pop pop
                (after special char: ) print =
        }{
                (no special chars found: ) =
        } ifelse
} bind def
```

Indentation Style

The single most important step you can take to make your program readable is to adopt a good indentation style. The PostScript language is very unstructured, and without proper indentation, it can be made quite impossible to read or maintain.

There are a few basic rules of indentation that you should observe, based on the structure of your program:

- Wherever one part of your program is contained within some clear beginning and ending constructs (such as **gsave** and **grestore**, **begin** and **end**, or curly braces), you should indent all of the included program text an equal amount.

- Use indentation to make it easy to find the beginning and ending of any matched construct visually.
- Be careful that adding and deleting lines from inside a structural element does not disturb the structure or readability of the program.

The indentation style used in the examples in this book is one developed over several years of maintaining programs, and it works well. There are other approaches, of course. The most common alternative to the method used in this book is to move the opening delimiters to a new line; this provides a much better balance, visually, to the delimiters, but it costs an extra line in the program (see Example 3.4). Extra lines don't consume much space, but editing a program is much easier when you can see more of the program at once in the screen of your text editor.

Example 3.4: Alternative Indentation Style for Procedures

```
/mapgray                          % -mapgray -
{ %def
        currentgray 0.5 gt
        { %ifelse
                1.0 setgray
        }
        { %else
                0.0 setgray
        } ifelse
} bind def
```

It is also a good idea to indent other program elements that have distinct beginning and endings, such as **begin** and **end** with dictionaries, **save** and **restore**, **gsave** and **grestore**, [and]. Example 3.5 shows some of these indentation styles in a dummy program.

Example 3.5: Indentation Style for Dictionaries and Structure

```
/mydict 24 dict def
mydict begin
        /draft                          % - draft -
        { %def
              /saveobj save def
                    500 600 moveto 10 rotate
                    /Helvetica 24 selectfont
                    0.5 setgray
                    gsave
                          (DRAFT) show
                    grestore
                    0 setgray 1 setlinewidth
                    (DRAFT) false charpath stroke
              saveobj restore
        } bind def
end %mydict
```

SETTING UP TEMPLATES

A very strong technique for building a structured PostScript program is to create an empty template for each construct in your program and then to go back and fill in the body of the template. This keeps you from having to remember to close all your delimiters and lets you perform your housekeeping all at once, so you can concentrate on other things. Anything that inherently has a beginning and an end will benefit from this technique, including making entries in a dictionary, creating an array, a procedure, a string, a loop, or a conditional.

The advantage to the template approach for **ifelse** statements, procedure definitions, loops, or other structural components is that you never have a partially written program with mismatched braces, which can be difficult to debug. The procedure body will already "work" when you finish with the template, although it may not do anything very interesting. At least you won't have a break in the structure of your program, even for the time it takes you to finish writing the procedure. Even if you are interrupted in the middle of building your **true** clause, the braces will still be balanced. It is also highly readable this way.

Example 3.6 shows how to lay out a template for a procedure definition, a dictionary, an array, an **ifelse** statement, and a loop. Once the template is in place, you can then come back to fill it in. The blank lines in the templates are where you add code later.

Example 3.6: Setting Up Templates

```
% dictionary template:
/mydict 24 dict def
mydict begin

end %mydict


% procedure template:
/newline                        % - newline -
{ %def
        % this procedure will simulate "newline"
        % on a line printer

} bind def

% conditional template:
currentgray 0.5 gt { %ifelse

}{ %else

} ifelse

% loop template:
0 10 360 { %for

} for


% combination template:
/mydict 24 dict def
mydict begin
        /newline                        % - newline -
        { %def
                currentpoint pop 550 gt { %ifelse
                }{ %else
                        0 10 360 { %for
                        } for
                } ifelse
        } bind def
end
```

Templates aren't just a learning tool, they are sound practice. The very best programmers use this technique every day, whether they are writing a simple example program for a book on PostScript or developing a quick hack to turn off the start page on the printer. Using templates will save you enormous amounts of time in the long run, and it is a highly recommended technique. If you learn nothing else from this book, please develop a habit of laying out templates as you program. Close those curly braces right after you open them, then go back and fill them in. Or, if you hate to use templates, at least develop your own techniques for laying out and maintaining the structure and indentation of the program source.

DECLARING AND USING VARIABLES

Variables serve two distinct purposes in a computer program. They provide a place to put data, especially data that might change, and they make the program much more readable than if you filled it up with numbers or string data. In PostScript, it is especially important to consider for which of these two purposes your variables were designed. In an interpreted language, you can pay a fairly high premium in execution time for only a little more readability.

There really is no such thing as a variable in PostScript, at least not in the sense that other languages have them. In C, for example, if you declare a variable of type **int**, the compiler will actually set aside a portion of memory big enough to hold an integer, and whenever you refer to that variable, the program knows to look in that location in memory. PostScript has no mechanism for declaring variables before they are used. It also does not require you to give names to any data structures. You can use data directly from the operand stack without ever storing the data into a variable, which you typically cannot do in other languages.

A variable in PostScript is just a name in a dictionary; what you really mean by "variable" probably is just a named bit of data. You refer to it by name instead of explicitly referring to the number or its location in memory. In that sense, any object can be a variable in a PostScript program, if you choose to define it in a dictionary. Let's look at a simple example (see Example 3.7).

Example 3.7: Declaring Variables

```
/LeftMargin 72 def
/TopMargin 792 72 sub def
/DocumentName (Thinking in PostScript) def
/ScaleFactor 300 72 div def
/DefaultFont /Courier findfont 12 scalefont def
```

In order to reference a variable, you simply use its name (without the slash). Whenever you use the name, the value will be looked up and executed. As long as the variable you have defined is not a procedure, the value of the variable will placed on the operand stack. In Example 3.8 you can see all the variables from Example 3.7 being used in some typical situations.

Example 3.8: Using Variables

```
ScaleFactor dup scale
LeftMargin TopMargin moveto
DefaultFont setfont
DocumentName show
```

Arithmetic with Numeric Variables

In most programming languages, you can easily perform arithmetic with variables, as in Example 3.9. But in the PostScript language, you have to do all your arithmetic on the operand stack, perhaps calling up the values of some variables to do so, then use the **def** operator to put the new value back into your variable. There is no operator that performs assignment like the = notation does in C. Example 3.10 shows the same arithmetic problems from Example 3.9 carried out in PostScript. Assume, of course, that in both examples all of the variables have been set up to contain reasonable values.

Example 3.9: Arithmetic in C

```
grade = (test1 + test2 + test3 + final ) / 4;
counter = counter + 1;
```

Example 3.10: Arithmetic in PostScript

```
/grade test1 test2 add test3 add final add 4 div def
/counter counter 1 add def
```

Remember, since all PostScript operators require their operands to be on the operand stack, the use of variables is never required. The same results can always be obtained using just the operand stack to hold your data. You can choose when you use a variable and when you don't.

Using the // Notation for Constants

PostScript has a special syntax for immediate name lookup and evaluation: the double slash. Any name that is preceded by a double slash (//) is looked up immediately when encountered in the program, even if it is inside a procedure body, where names are not normally looked up until the procedure is executed.

One excellent use of this notation is to set up constants that you want to work like variables but will never change. That way you can obtain the readability of having named variables, but when the program executes, they will actually be replaced by their constant value and the name lookup at run-time will be avoided. For a simple illustration of this technique, see Example 3.11.

Example 3.11: Evaluation of Constants with //

```
/LeftMargin 108 def                  % constant definitions
/TopMargin 792 72 sub def
/RightMargin 612 72 sub def
/BottomMargin 72 def
/Leading 12 def
/space                      % - space -
{ %def
        currentpoint exch //RightMargin gt { %ifelse
                //Leading sub dup //BottomMargin lt { %ifelse
                        pop showpage
                        //LeftMargin //TopMargin moveto
                }{ %else
                        //LeftMargin exch moveto
                } ifelse
        }{ pop } ifelse
} bind def
```

Notice that all of the variables for margins and leading are used with the double slash notation inside the procedure body. The names are there for you to look at when you are editing the program, but when it is executed, they are replaced by their numeric values inside the body of the procedure before the procedure is ever encountered. In fact, if you look at the procedure body on the stack right before **bind** is executed, you will see a procedure that looks quite a bit different than the one in your source program. (For instance, compare Example 3.11 and Example 3.12).

Example 3.12: After Immediate Name Lookup with //

```
/LeftMargin 108 def                  % constant definitions
/TopMargin 792 72 sub def
/RightMargin 612 72 sub def
/BottomMargin 72 def
/Leading 12 def
/space                    % - space -
{ %def
        currentpoint exch 540 gt { %ifelse
                12 sub dup 72 lt { %ifelse
                        pop showpage
                        108 720 moveto
                }{ %else
                        108 exch moveto
                } ifelse
        }{ pop } ifelse
} bind def
```

NOTE: The // syntax for immediate name lookup is not available in the very first implementations of a PostScript interpreter, which are those with version numbers below 25.0 from Adobe Systems Incorporated.

ALLOCATING MEMORY

There are two ways that memory gets allocated in a PostScript program. It is either allocated implicitly when an object is created or it is allocated explicitly by using one of a handful of operators that create empty data structures of a particular size. See Table 3.1 for a list of operators that explicitly allocate memory for data storage.

Table 3.1: Operators that Explicitly Allocate Memory

Arguments	Operator	Action
int **array** *array*		create *array* of length *int*
int **dict** *dict*		create empty dictionary with capacity for *int* elements
matrix *matrix*		create identity *matrix*
any_0 ... any_{n-1} int **packedarray** *packarr*		create packed array consisting of specified *int* elements
int **string** *string*		create empty *string* of length *int*

The operators in Table 3.1, with the exception of **matrix**, all take an integer argument specifying exactly how large a data structure to allocate. The **matrix** operator always creates an array with six elements, and is equivalent to the code sequence [**1 0 0 1 0 0**].

There are also a number of ways to allocate memory implicitly, sometimes without even realizing it. In general, whenever a composite object is created, memory must be allocated to store its contents. There are a few operators that create composite objects implicitly, and a few bits of PostScript language syntax that will cause a composite object to be created. These operations are summarized in Table 3.2.

Table 3.2: Implicit Memory Allocation

Arguments	Operator	Action
[obj_0 ... obj_{n-1}]	array	create a literal array
{ any_0 ... any_n }	proc	create an executable array
(*any bytes*)		create a string body
<*hex bytes*>		create hexadecimal string body
gstate *gstate_obj*		create a new gstate object
save *save_obj*		create a new save object

The most common of these methods for implicitly allocating memory are procedure bodies and strings. The latter would *literal strings*, if they are created by the PostScript interpreter when it recognizes a string represented with the ( ) notation.

A composite object, whether created explicitly or implicitly, uses memory in proportion to its size. For example, when you create a dictionary object, a certain amount of memory is allocated for each entry in the dictionary, and the total amount allocated depends on how many empty slots are in the dictionary to be created. Similarly, a string object will require more memory if the string is a long one. In either case, the memory allocated is exact, and should be predictable. A string that is thirty bytes long requires exactly ten bytes more storage than a string that is twenty bytes long.

This discussion does not cover the precise details of memory allocation, but it does provide a pretty good framework for understanding how memory is consumed in a PostScript program. If you are concerned about gaining precise control over memory allocation, it is best to get specific documentation for the interpreter that you are using.

GETTING MEMORY BACK

Once you have allocated memory in your program, either by creating data structures or by executing some code that uses memory, there are only two ways to reclaim that space:

- Use the **save** and **restore** operators to reclaim all memory used since the last **save** was executed.
- Use the **undef**, **undefinefont**, and **vmreclaim** operators available in the Display PostScript extensions to the PostScript language (*not available in all products*).

When using **save** and **restore**, you have to plan carefully where you want to restore the contents of memory, because the **save/restore** mechanism also affects other aspects of the interpreter, including the current graphic state, the current device, and so on. In a typical page description, **save** and **restore** may be done at each page boundary or around each page element (like a block of text or a photographic image).

OPENING AND CLOSING FILES

Opening and closing files is a fundamental operation in any program, which is why this section is included in this chapter on the basics. The quick overview is that there are a lot of file-related PostScript operators for reading and writing files; there is one for opening files (the **file** operator) and one for closing files (the **closefile** operator). The **file** operator returns a *file object* that you must retain for all subsequent file operations (including **closefile**). Please see Chapter 14 for a complete discussion of file operations.

COMPARISONS AND EQUALITY OF OBJECTS

PostScript has several distinct data types and is fairly strict about type-checking. However, you can easily convert one type to another, assuming that the type conversion makes some sense, and you can then compare them. (See Data Conversions in Chapter 13 for a discussion of type conversions.) In many instances, the PostScript comparison operators will even do this for you as a convenience. Strings and names, for example, are both simply composed of bytes, so they can easily be compared, as shown in Example 3.13.

Example 3.13: Comparison of Different Types of Objects

```
% comparing reals with integers:
103.0 103 eq            % true
103.0 103 ge            % true
103.0 103 gt            % false

% comparing mark objects:
mark [ eq               % true

% comparing null objects to integers and booleans:
null 0 eq               % false
null false eq           % false

% comparing strings and name objects:
(Palatino-Roman)
/Palatino-Roman eq      % true
(abc)
(defabc)
3 3 getinterval eq      % true
(abc) (abc) eq          % true (an exception)

% comparing array objects:
[ 1 2 3 ] dup eq        % true
[ 1 2 3 ]
[ 1 2 3 ] eq            % false (arrays created independently)
matrix matrix eq        % false
{ 1 exch sub }
{ 1 exch sub } eq       % false

% comparing dictionary objects:
5 dict dup begin
currentdict eq          % true
```

```
/show where { %if
        systemdict eq          % true (if "show" has not been redefined)
} if
5 dict 5 dict eq               % false (dictionaries created independently)

% comparing file objects:
(%stdin) (r) file
currentfile eq                 % true (most of the time)

% comparing operator objects:
{ 1 2 add } bind 2 get
/add load eq                   % true (if "add" has not been redefined)
```

As you may have noticed upon careful reading of Example 3.13, some
composite objects (dictionaries, procedures, and arrays) get a little bit
tricky when you compare them. In particular, when you use, say, the **eq**
operator, you are comparing the objects themselves, not the structure to
which they point. Composite objects represent a structure that is stored in
memory somewhere. If you create two different structures, even if they
happen to contain the same elements, the structures themselves are
independent, and therefore the objects that represent them are not
considered to be equal. However, if you have two copies of the same
composite object, the **eq** operator will confirm that they are in fact equal.

Example 3.14: Procedure to Compare Array Contents

```
/arrayeq                    % array1 array2 arrayeq bool
{ %def
      2 copy eq { pop pop true }{ %ifelse
                % if lengths are not equal, return false
                2 copy length exch length eq { %ifelse
                    % We now have to compare all elements
                    true                      % arr arr true
                    0 1 3 index length 1 sub { %for
                            3 index 1 index get   % arr arr bool index val1
                            3 index 2 index get   % arr arr bool index val1 val2
                            eq exch pop and       % arr arr bool
                    } for
                    exch pop exch pop
                }{ pop pop false } ifelse
      } ifelse
} bind def
/arrayne { arrayeq not } bind def
```

If you really need to find out if two independently formed composite objects are equivalent, you can compare their contents. If their contents are exactly equal and the lengths of the two composite objects are equal, then you can consider the two composite objects to be *equivalent*, if not equal. In Example 3.14 is a procedure definition called **arrayeq** that will compare two arrays, returning **true** if their contents and lengths are equal.

CONCLUDING THOUGHTS

If you build a solid foundation of PostScript programming skills, you should be able to write programs that work the very first time. There isn't much to forget, really. You don't have to declare variables, the syntax is very free, and you cannot get compile-time errors. It helps to get the indentation right, so that all of the parentheses and curly braces balance correctly, and if you develop the skill of always laying out a template for a structure before you go back and fill it in, you should never run into that problem.

The next chapter provides a few examples of typical PostScript programs to help you adopt a style and structure that is appropriate for the task you are faced with. A program to render a graph on a laser printer may be quite different from a program that constructs a downloadable font, for example, and the programming techniques you use should reflect the task.

EXERCISES

1. Syntax errors arise very infrequently in PostScript, but when they do, it can be difficult to track them down.

   a. Find the syntax error in the following program segment:

   ```
   0 1 20 { ( Hello world (part 1) == flush } for
   ```

   b. Find the syntax error in the following program segment:

   ```
   currentpoint exch 32 gt {
           72 lt { showpage 36 500 moveto
   } if { %else
           (hello world \(part 2) show
   } ifelse
   ```

2. Create a simple procedure named **line** that takes four operands, the *x, y* location for the beginning of the line and the *x, y* location for the end of the line. The procedure should perform the necessary **moveto**, **lineto**, and **stroke** operations. Use your procedure once or twice to create some sample lines.

3. Create a template for a procedure that contains an **ifelse** statement.

4. Design a procedure called **++** that will increment a variable. The procedure should be able to increment any variable that contains an integer or a real value. Design it so that the following sample will add **1** to the value of the variable named **counter** each time it is called:

```
/counter 0 def
/counter ++
/counter ++
counter ==       % should be 2
```

Chapter 4

Some Typical Programs

This chapter presents some of the most common variations in PostScript programs. It provides you with a glimpse of different programming styles and lets you know when they might be appropriate. Not all PostScript programs draw pictures or print pages. Some of them are purely utilitarian, some are exploratory, some may delete files from your desk, download a font, or query a printer for a list of built-in typefaces.

A lot has been written about PostScript page descriptions, since that was the original purpose of the language. Many of the recommended techniques and program structural rules were intended mostly for page descriptions. Part of the purpose of showing some other kinds of programs is to address squarely the issue of creating PostScript programs that are not simply documents.

The samples in this chapter are not necessarily intended for you to copy as great programming examples. The idea is to present several different classes of programs, to point out that the programming style and the problems faced may differ dramatically between, say, a font program and an Encapsulated PostScript program (which is explained later in this chapter).

A TYPICAL PAGE DESCRIPTION PROGRAM

Although PostScript is a full-featured programming language, its primary purpose was originally for page description. In this sense, the program is only the means to an end. The point of a page description is purely graphical, and the marks on the page or on the screen are the intent; the program's role is to facilitate the rendering of graphics.

Let's look at a very simplistic page description from a programming point of view. Typically page descriptions are produced by a document processing application, and are not generally written by hand. Machine-generated PostScript programs always have some amount of hand-tuned code, especially in the procedure definitions, but the body of the document is usually generated directly by the document production system.

For instance, if you wrote a drawing program that allows the user to draw boxes, you might create a PostScript procedure to help you draw boxes efficiently, but this procedure would be very general, and would require information about where to draw the box and how big it should be. This data would be supplied by the drawing program itself, based on the boxes drawn by the user. The box procedure would then be invoked as many times as necessary to render all the boxes drawn by the user.

Since documents can be composed of many, many elements, and since the set of possible graphic elements is normally fixed, it makes sense to make the representation for each individual object as compact and efficient as possible, using the ability to define procedures as a mechanism. Example 4.1 shows the output of a fictitious text-setting application, with a typical blend of procedure definitions and invocations in the body of the document; Figure 4.1 shows the text generated by the code.

Example 4.1: Sample Page Description Program

```
%!PS-Adobe-2.1
%%Title: sample document
%%Creator: textset v-1.0
%%DocumentFonts: Times-Roman Times-Italic
%%BoundingBox: 0 0 612 792
%%Pages: 2
%%EndComments
%%BeginProcSet: textset 1.0 0
        /selectfont where { %ifelse
                pop
        }{ %else
                /selectfont { %def
                        exch findfont exch scalefont setfont
                } bind def
        /F /selectfont load def
        /T { moveto show } bind def
%%EndProcSet
%%EndProlog
%%Page: 1 1
        /Times-Roman 24 F
        (Now is the time for all good) 72 72 T
        /Times-Italic 24 F
        (people) 349 72 T
        /Times-Roman 24 F
        (to come) 416 72 T
         (to the aid of their country.) 72 46 T
        showpage
%%Page: 2 2
        /Times-Roman 24 F
        (Now is the time for all good) 72 72 T
        /Times-Italic 24 F
        (people) 349 72 T
        /Times-Roman 24 F
        (to come) 416 72 T
         (to the aid of their country.) 72 46 T
        showpage
%%Trailer
```

Figure 4.1: Output from Example 4.1

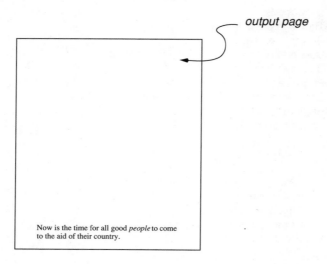

output page

Now is the time for all good *people* to come
to the aid of their country.

There are several things that affect the programming style in page descriptions. First, there is usually a great deal of structure in the program, and in fact the whole program can be thought of as a document containing pages, illustrations, and so on. In Example 4.1, the structure is delineated according to document structuring conventions, where comments like **%%EndProlog** mark the boundaries between the elements of the document. In this case, there are really only two major components, known as the *prologue* and the *script*. The prologue is simply a few PostScript language definitions that permit more powerful and compact representations to be made in the document. The script is the body of the document, and contains mostly data from the document processing system such as fonts, locations on the page, and bits of text. The prologue is usually the same for all documents, and is hand-written, whereas the script is generated by the document processing program.

FONT PROGRAMS

A font program is simply a PostScript program that creates a font dictionary and registers it as a font. Since it is a program, there is no required font file format to adhere to. The dictionary structure of the font is important, but it can be built in a variety of ways. (See the *PostScript Language Reference Manual* for a complete specification of the required font dictionary structure.) Example 4.2 is a very minimal program that illustrates the structure of a font program. The characters in this font draw completely random line segments (see Figure 4.2); its practical merit is questionable.

Example 4.2: Sample Font Program

```
%%BeginFont: UserFont
 14 dict begin
      /FontName /UserFont def
      /FontType 3 def
      /FontMatrix [ .001 0 0 .001 0 0 ] def
      /FontBoundingBox [ 0 0 1000 1000 ] def
      /Encoding /StandardEncoding load def
      /BuildChar                    % fontdict charcode BuildChar -
      { %def
            exch begin
                  Encoding exch get
                  500 0 setcharwidth
                  CharDefs exch get exec
            end
      } bind def
      /CharDefs 256 dict def
      CharDefs begin
            Encoding { %forall
                  { %def
                        4 { rand 1000 mod } repeat
                        moveto lineto stroke
                  } def
            } bind forall
      end
 currentdict end dup /FontName get exch definefont pop
%%EndFont
/UserFont 48 selectfont
10 10 moveto (abcdefg) show
showpage
```

Figure 4.2: Output from Example 4.2

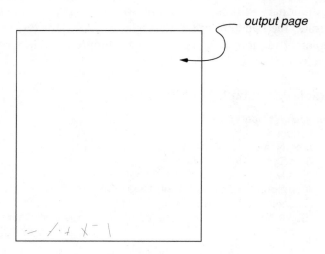

output page

PROGRAMS THAT READ DATA

One of the most common operations in a computer program is to read and write data from a file. In the past, most PostScript programs have not had access to a file system anywhere other than on the printer, if the printer happened to have a hard disk attached. In window system environments based on PostScript, it is much more likely that a file system is available.

Example 4.3: Sample Program that Reads Data

```
%!PS-Adobe-2.0
%%Title: data reading example
/infile (input.ps) (r) file def
/outfile (output.ps) (w) file def
/buffer 128 string def
{ %loop
        infile buffer readstring { %ifelse
                outfile exch writestring
        } {      outfile exch writestring exit } ifelse
} bind loop
infile closefile outfile closefile
```

The program in Example 4.3 reads lines from one text file and writes them to another output file; in other words, it just copies the file.

QUERY PROGRAMS

Sometimes you need to retrieve some information about a printer or network server, like a list of the currently installed fonts. This is an example of a *query program*. Query programs always generate a response of some kind as part of their execution. Example 4.4 is a query program that returns a list of the fonts currently defined in the **FontDirectory** dictionary in a PostScript interpreter.

Example 4.4: Sample Query Program

```
%!PS-Adobe-2.0 Query
%%EndComments
%?BeginFontListQuery
FontDirectory { pop == } forall flush
(*) = flush
%?EndFontListQuery: *
```

Since query programs are intended to write results to the *standard output* communications channel (terminology borrowed from UNIX and C), their behavior depends to a great degree upon the environment in which they are executed. Some printers do not have two-way communications channels; in such cases the results will be lost. Some operating environments think that anything coming back from a printer must be an error message, so the results may be written to an error log file somewhere, and they may even have extra text added to them by the printer control program.

ENCAPSULATED POSTSCRIPT PROGRAMS

Encapsulated PostScript files (EPS files) are illustrations or other self-contained programs that can be included into another document. They are restricted in a few ways to keep them from disturbing the environment in which they are included, but generally can use the entire expressive power of the PostScript language (see Example 4.5).

Example 4.5: Sample Encapsulated PostScript Program

```
/EPSsave save def
.25 .25 scale .7 .7 scale 200 200 translate 20 rotate
/showpage { } def
% begin included EPS file
%!PS-Adobe-2.0 EPSF-1.2
%%Title: EPSF example program
%%BoundingBox: 100 100 500 500
%%DocumentFonts: Palatino-BoldItalic
%%EndComments
%%BeginProcSet: adobe_DPSrectanglepack 1.0
/rectfill where { pop }{ %ifelse
        /*buildrect {
                dup type /integertype eq 1 index type /realtype eq or { %ifelse
                        4 -2 roll moveto dup 0 exch rlineto
                        exch 0 rlineto neg 0 exch rlineto
                        closepath
                }{ %else
                        dup type /arraytype eq {
                                aload length 4 div cvi { %repeat
                                        *buildrect
                                } repeat
                        } if
                } ifelse
        } bind def
        /rectfill { %def
                gsave *buildrect fill grestore
        } bind def
        /rectstroke { %def
                gsave *buildrect stroke grestore
        } bind def
        /rectclip { %def
                newpath *buildrect clip newpath
        } bind def
} ifelse
%%EndProcSet: adobe_DPSrectanglepack 1.0
%%EndProlog
gsave
        .75 setgray 100 100 500 500 rectfill
        0 setgray 3 setlinewidth 100 100 500 500 rectstroke
grestore
120 400 moveto /Palatino-BoldItalic findfont 75 scalefont setfont
gsave (Encapsulated) show grestore 0 -100 rmoveto
(PostScript) show
% end included EPS file
EPSsave restore
```

In Figure 4.3 you can see the output of Example 4.5; it has been scaled smaller, translated to another position on the page, and rotated 20 degrees. All of these changes reflect the way EPS files are typically used, and are designed to reinforce the fact that the code in an Encapsulated PostScript file should not disturb the environment into which it is placed.

Figure 4.3: Output from Example 4.5

The specification for Encapsulated PostScript files allows for an optional preview component of the file, to accommodate weak display systems that cannot execute the PostScript code directly. This preview component is usually a bit map in a format appropriate to the native environment on which the document was created (it may be a Macintosh PICT resource, for example). The preview component of an Encapsulated PostScript file is strictly optional and is in no way connected to the PostScript code, except that it is supposed to represent the same picture.

PERSISTENTLY RESIDENT PROGRAMS

Yet another type of PostScript program is one that makes some persistent definitions that are visible to all subsequent programs. This provides a mechanism for redefining operators, making fonts semipermanent in the interpreter, or defining some procedure definitions once in such a way that they are usable to all subsequent programs.

On most printer implementations, this can be accomplished using the **exitserver** operator. This operator permits the program to exit the job server loop's **save/restore** context, causing any definitions made to stay resident until the printer is rebooted. Example 4.6 shows the use of **exitserver**, in this case to make a font definition semipermanent.

Example 4.6: Sample Printer-Resident Program

```
%!PS-Adobe-2.0 ExitServer
%%EndComments
%%BeginExitServer: 0
      serverdict begin 0 exitserver
%%EndExitServer
%%BeginFont: UserFont
 13 dict begin
      /FontName /UserFont def /FontType 3 def
      /FontMatrix [ .001 0 0 .001 0 0 ] def
      /FontBoundingBox [ 0 0 1000 1000 ] def
      /Encoding /StandardEncoding load def
      /BuildChar                 % fontdict charcode BuildChar -
      { %def
            exch begin
                  Encoding exch get 500 0 setcharwidth
                  CharDefs exch get exec
            end
      } bind def
      /CharDefs 256 dict def CharDefs begin
            Encoding { %forall
                  { %def
                              4 { rand 1000 mod } repeat moveto lineto stroke
                  } def
            } bind forall
      end
 currentdict end dup /FontName get exch definefont pop
%%EndFont
%%EOF
```

In window system environments, the concept of a job server loop is often not present, since a windowed environment is usually not a batch system. With the Display PostScript System, there is a dictionary called **shareddict**, in which all entries are shared by all processes (and hence visible to all). Example 4.7 shows the same font definition made permanent or public in Display PostScript. Notice the use of the **currentshared** and **setshared** operators.

Example 4.7: Sample Display-Server-Resident Program

```
%!PS-Adobe-2.0 ExitServer
%%EndComments
%%BeginExitServer: 0
dup 0 eq { pop } if true setshared
%%EndExitServer
%%BeginFont: UserFont
 13 dict begin
      /FontName /UserFont def /FontType 3 def
      /FontMatrix [ .001 0 0 .001 0 0 ] def
      /FontBoundingBox [ 0 0 1000 1000 ] def
      /Encoding /StandardEncoding load def
      /BuildChar                % fontdict charcode BuildChar -
      { %def
            exch begin
                  Encoding exch get
                  500 0 setcharwidth
                  CharDefs exch get exec
            end
      } bind def
      /CharDefs 256 dict def CharDefs begin
            Encoding { %forall
                  { %def
                              4 { rand 1000 mod } repeat
                              moveto lineto stroke
                  } def
            } bind forall
      end
 currentdict end dup /FontName get exch definefont pop
%%EndFont
%%EOF
```

TIP The **exitserver** operator is not a standard part of the language. It is defined in most printers, but is usually not implemented in display servers or stand-alone interpreters. In general, use of **exitserver** is restricted to system administrators. It should never be part of the output of a program, nor should it be used routinely in any program.

Figure 4.4: Shared Memory Configuration

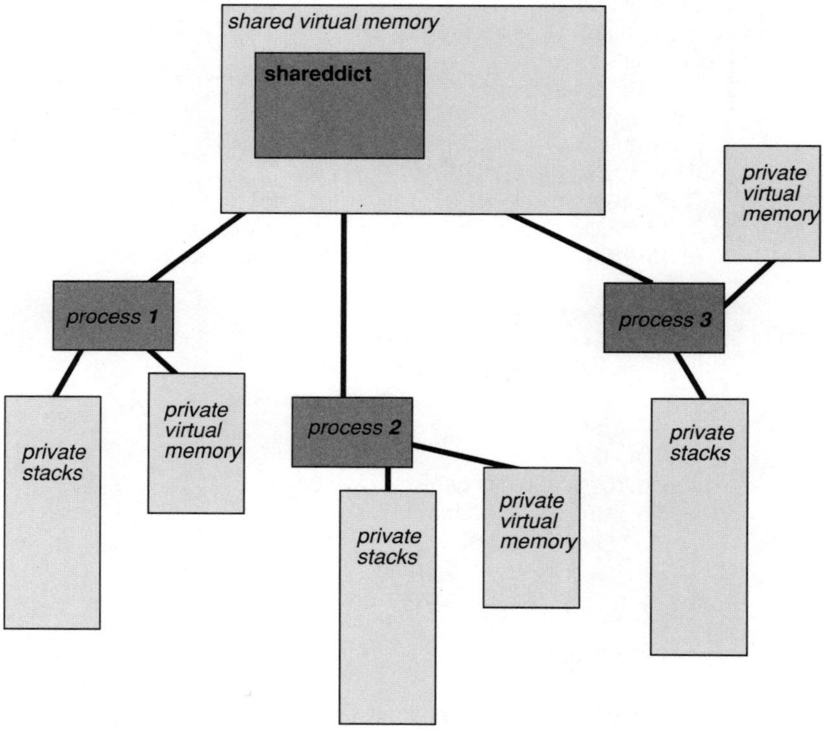

Figure 4.4 provides an illustration of the concept of shared virtual memory (often referred to as VM).

CONCLUDING THOUGHTS

The examples in this chapter should provide a feeling for the different kinds of programs that can be written, and the different techniques that might be required for each. As you learn more about the details of writing PostScript programs, it is helpful to keep a bit of perspective about the kind of program you are constructing, so you can make your code readable where it should be, efficient where it counts, and well-behaved. The next two chapters take a hard look at the operand stack, since it is the principle mechanism for all program execution.

EXERCISES

1. In a page description program, is it more important to write code that is easily readable or code that is efficient? What kinds of procedures would you define, and why?

2. What kinds of PostScript programs would you expect to consume memory?

3. What do you think is a reasonable way to use a query program in an environment where there is only one-way communication (or in a batch system, which is essentially the same thing) ?

Chapter 5

Understanding the Stack

The operand stack is the central mechanism in the PostScript language. All data are placed on the operand stack at one time or another during the execution of your program. The operand stack holds PostScript language *objects*, which are the basic representation for all data types in a PostScript program, including procedures and instructions.

A QUICK OVERVIEW OF DATA TYPES

All PostScript data types are represented by a single object. There are three varieties: *simple* objects like integers, reals, marks, and booleans; *composite* objects (like arrays and strings) that will not fit into an object; and some *special* types that behave like simple objects but which have some internal structure that you can't see (these include save objects and **FontID** objects). For the purpose of this discussion, only simple and composite objects will be covered.

Data types are represented in the interpreter as *objects*, which are a fixed size and are easily manipulated by the interpreter, placed on the operand stack, or stored into arrays or dictionaries. For the most part, it is not necessary to know that data types are represented as objects, but it does affect some things. For a more complete discussion of PostScript language objects and data types, please refer to the *PostScript Language Reference Manual*.

Probably the most important distinction to understand between the various data types is the difference between a simple object and a composite object. Composite objects can be thought of as pointers to the real data, whereas simple objects really are data themselves. Figure 5.1 shows the various data types available in PostScript.

Figure 5.1: PostScript Data Types, Simple and Composite

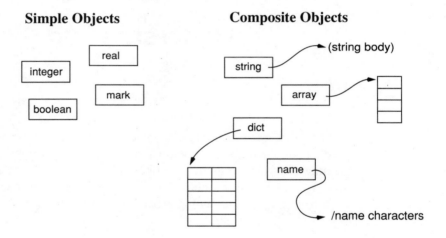

PostScript objects are created in one of two ways: they are either created directly by the language interpreter when it reads the program from the input file, or they are created directly by the executing program itself through an explicit allocation. Some data types (the real number is an example) cannot be created explicitly by a program except by converting another data type (an integer). It must be created by the scanner, as it reads a number from the input stream (for instance, 103.46). Other data types cannot be created at all by the scanner. For example, the data types mark and boolean are created by the PostScript operators **mark**, **true**, or **false**, or as side effects of some other operators such as **known** or **search**.

NAME LOOKUP

The standard method for retrieving something that has been stored into a dictionary is to use the *name lookup* mechanism. An executable name encountered by the interpreter is looked up in the context of the current dictionary stack, and if there is an entry corresponding to that name, the value will be placed on the operand stack—with one notable exception. If you happen to retrieve a procedure body (an executable array object) under the name you look up, that procedure will be placed on the execution stack and immediately executed, rather than being placed on the operand stack and treated as data.

TIP

If you need to retrieve a procedure body that you have stored into a dictionary, but don't want to execute it just yet, you can get a copy of it onto the operand stack using the **load** operator, using the name of your procedure (with the leading slash, to make it a literal name) as the argument to **load**.

When a name is looked up, the dictionary stack is searched from the top down, and the first instance of the key that is encountered is the one that is used. That enables you to redefine a name that is already built into the PostScript language, although you should do so with great care (see Redefining Operators in Chapter 10 for further discussion of this topic).

HOW OPERATORS USE THE STACK

The *operand stack* is a global communication area for all PostScript programs. All operators look for their operands on the stack and produce results there, although they may also produce side effects such as marks on the page, changes to the graphics state, or changes to the contents of memory.

Let's look at a very simple program to follow the use of the operand stack (See Example 5.1).

Example 5.1: Simple Use of the Operand Stack

```
/Times-Roman 12 selectfont
/Xlocation 100 def
/Ylocation 200 def
Xlocation Ylocation moveto
(text sample) show
```

This code segment looks like a definition of two variables, **Xlocation** and **Ylocation**, which are then used as the coordinates for the **moveto** operator. From the point of view of stack manipulation, the **def** operator simply takes two objects from the stack and puts them in the current dictionary, and the subsequent name lookup of, say, **Xlocation**, retrieves the object associated with that key from the current dictionary. As shown in Figure 5.2, by the time you get to **moveto**, there are no variables or anything else left; there are just two numbers on the operand stack, which is what is required by the **moveto** operator. So in effect, the numbers **100** and **200** start out on the operand stack, are stored into a dictionary, retrieved from that dictionary back onto the operand stack, and used by the **moveto** instruction. A variable is a name used to reference data.

TIP

When you define a variable in your PostScript program, you are actually taking something off the operand stack and putting it into a dictionary. In order to use the variable, you must always recall it from the dictionary back onto the operand stack. Be aware that using "variables" is always somewhat slower than using the operand stack directly.

To understand how the operand stack works, it is worthwhile to step through a simple program, executing it in your head. It is important enough that you might spend some real time at this, until you are extremely comfortable talking through a program, understanding exactly what happens to it as it is being executed.

Figure 5.2: Tracing the Execution of Example 5.1

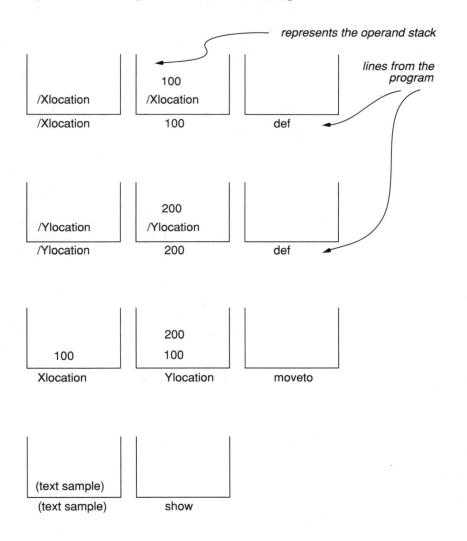

All PostScript operators expect their operands in a particular, fixed order. For example, the **put** operator requires the following operands:

compositeobject index value put

If you mix up the index and the value, you will very likely get an error, although not always, if the values are still within range. Remember that the PostScript operators themselves don't know what you have in mind. They are flexible, and will allow you to do things that you may not have intended. It is very easy to lose track of what is on the operand stack, or to supply incorrect operands to some operator, leading to bugs in your program that are sometimes difficult to locate.

GROUPING AND VISUAL CHUNKING

One of the best ways to learn to read and write PostScript programs is to be able to "chunk" together sequences of instructions into a block that has a well-understood input and output. In many programming languages, you can usually read a single line of the source code and make sense of it. In fact, usually one line of the program represents a single *statement* in that language, which may be an assignment statement or a procedure call. But in the PostScript language, the statements can get fairly complex, and each operator and its arguments represents one phrase of the statement. The programs that are the most difficult to read are those that use one operator to manufacture the arguments for the next operator.

Let's look quickly at two examples that illustrate the concept of one operator leaving behind results that become arguments for the subsequent operation. The first case (Example 5.2) shows a series of code samples of gradually increasing complexity, culminating in some that may look a little bit confusing at first glance. Take a moment to mentally execute the program to see what it does.

Example 5.2: Each Operator Uses the Operand Stack

```
% currentgray leaves result for setgray
currentgray 1 exch sub setgray

% save leaves a value for restore ("3 exch" is just there to confuse you)
save 3 exch restore

% search leaves three strings and a boolean
(ABCD) (B) search { = pop = flush }{ = flush } ifelse
```

Example 5.3 is an extremely familiar program fragment that is actually somewhat tricky in its operation. The **findfont** operator returns a dictionary that is used by the **scalefont** operator, and if you ever mix up the order of these operators, you might never even know that this object was there, since it no sooner is produced than it is consumed again. The **(Testing) exch** part of this example demonstrates that there really is a font dictionary on the operand stack, and if you put something else on top of it and use **exch** to flip the two, **scalefont** will still have the right information on the stack to perform its task, but the string will now be on the bottom of the stack, ready to be used by **show** at the end of the example.

Example 5.3: The *findfont* Operator Returns a Dictionary

```
/Times-Roman findfont (Testing) exch 12 scalefont setfont show
```

The secret to "visual chunking" is to recognize an operator and its operands in the middle of a program segment. You might have noticed several candidates for visual chunking in the short program of Example 5.3. Even if you didn't, with a little practice, you'll learn to chunk program fragments together visually, greatly improving your ability to read PostScript code. There are really three kinds of things you can see:

1. A sequence of operators that, combined, yields a new object or group of objects on the operand stack.
2. A sequence of operators that may rearrange or duplicate some elements of the stack, but which do not inherently add anything new to the stack.
3. Operations that consume or otherwise remove things from the operand stack.

Visual chunking for the code of Example 5.3 is illustrated graphically in Figure 5.3.

After a while, you start to see bigger chunks all at once, which makes it much easier to follow the program.

Figure 5.3: Visual Chunking for Example 5.3

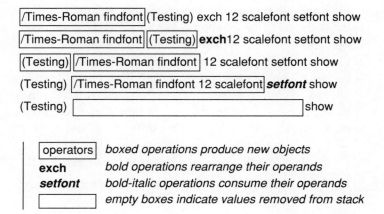

THINKING BACKWARD AND SIDEWAYS
==============================

A stack-based language such as PostScript makes you think differently than most programming languages. It seems, at first, as though you have to think backwards, since all the operators come after their operands. However, if you think of the entire expression at once, it is only slightly different than thinking in prefix or infix notation (see Example 5.4 through Example 5.6).

Example 5.4: Operator Prefix Notation in C

```
/* In a function call, the operands come in parentheses after the function name */
value = currentpoint(Y);
value = sqrt(X);
```

Example 5.5: Operator Infix Notation in C

```
/* Arithmetic operators typically come between their operands */
value = value - 12;
if ( value <= 72 ) showpage();
```

Example 5.6: Postfix Notation in PostScript

```
% In PostScript, the operators always come after the operands:
currentpoint exch pop 72 lt { showpage } if
```

Since the PostScript language allows you to write programs in a very open format, the emphasis on backward thinking is even less, and sideways thinking becomes more important, such as in Example 5.7. The language would feel much more stack-oriented if you were forced to write only one token on each line, more like assembly language. That is, in fact, almost exactly what the interpreter sees, since it reads a single token and acts on it before reading the next token.

Example 5.7: Programming One Token at a Time

```
/Times-Roman
findfont
(Testing)
exch
12
scalefont
setfont
show
```

In reality, the most common occurrence is a combination of horizontal and vertical thinking. Consider the common case of a procedure that uses local names for its arguments (Example 5.8). Its output is shown in Figure 5.4 for your reference.

Example 5.8: Procedure Arguments on the Stack

```
/graybox                    % gray linewidth Lx Ly Ux Uy graybox -
{ %def
        /upperY exch def
        /upperX exch def
        /lowerY exch def
        /lowerX exch def
        /linewidth exch def
        /gray exch def
        lowerX lowerY moveto
        lowerX upperY lineto
        upperX upperY lineto
        upperX lowerY lineto closepath
```

```
    gsave
            gsave gray setgray fill grestore
            linewidth setlinewidth stroke
    grestore
} bind def
0.5 2 100 200 500 400 graybox
```

Figure 5.4: Output of Example 5.8

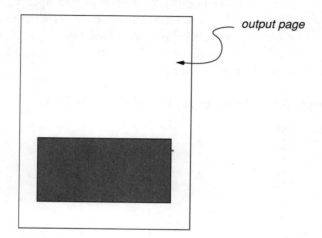

output page

Since stacks are *last-in, first-out* data structures, the last object on a line is at the very top of the operand stack. In this example, this can be seen most clearly by looking at the procedure call itself; that's why the first line in the procedure grabs the last argument on the line, since it is now on the top of the operand stack (see Figure 5.5).

You can start to see the relationship in this example between the left-to-right distribution of objects in the source program and the top-to-bottom result on the operand stack. Notice the way the arguments to the procedure line up with the **exch def** lines in the procedure definition itself.

TIP　　　When reading a PostScript program, find the *executable names* and use them as reference points. If the name is a procedure call, look to the left of the name in the body of the program to follow along as you read down through the procedure definition (as in Figure 5.5).

Figure 5.5: Last Object In is the First Out

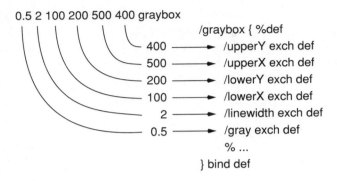

0.5 2 100 200 500 400 graybox

/graybox { %def
400 ——→ /upperY exch def
500 ——→ /upperX exch def
200 ——→ /lowerY exch def
100 ——→ /lowerX exch def
2 ——→ /linewidth exch def
0.5 ——→ /gray exch def
% ...
} bind def

COMPOSITE OBJECTS

The values associated with composite objects do not exist on the operand stack. There is an object on the stack that represents the composite object data, and it behaves, for the most part, as though the whole object were on the stack. The only time it is confusing is during copying and manipulation of the internal structure of a composite object, when you have to realize that you really have a pointer to the object, not a self-contained object. For example, if you **dup** a string object and then change one of the letters in the copied object, the original string changes, too, since there really is only one string and you have only copied the pointer to it, not the string itself.

Figure 5.6: Duplicating a Composite Object

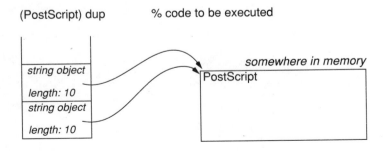

(PostScript) dup   % code to be executed

string object
length: 10
string object
length: 10

somewhere in memory
PostScript

The illustration in Figure 5.6 gives you an idea of what happens when you duplicate a composite object like a string. All stack manipulations to composite objects operate on the single object, not on the entire body of the composite data. In this example there are two string pointers on the operand stack that have the same value. If one of these is changed, they are both changed, as can be seen in Figure 5.7.

Figure 5.7: Changing a Composite Object

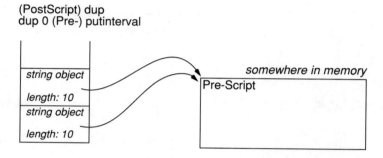

```
(PostScript) dup
dup 0 (Pre-) putinterval
```

THE OTHER STACKS

There are three other stacks used by the interpreter during the execution of your program in addition to the operand stack, which you have been studying: the *dictionary stack*, which helps with name lookup and in making definitions; the *execution stack*, which holds partially executed procedure bodies, file objects, and other executable objects; and the *graphics state stack*, which keeps track of your **gsave** and **grestore** operations.

These stacks will be described briefly so that you'll know about them. For more detailed information, refer to the books *PostScript Language Reference Manual* and *PostScript Language Program Design*, both by Adobe Systems, available from Addison-Wesley Publishing Company.

The Dictionary Stack

The dictionary stack controls name lookup and dictates where an entry is made when you use the **def** operator. You can only place dictionary objects onto this stack, and only with the **begin** operator. You must use the **end** operator to remove entries from the dictionary stack. There is also a discussion of these operations in the section entitled Maintaining the Dictionary Stack in Chapter 10.

The Execution Stack

The execution stack is used only internally by the interpreter, to keep track of your program's execution. It contains any portion of the program that has not yet been executed, including the input file stream, any partially-executed procedure bodies, and loops. There are very few ways to take advantage of the execution stack in a user program, but it can help in complicated debugging situations.

The Graphics State Stack

The graphics state stack is used only by the **gsave** and **grestore** operators to maintain the graphics state. The gsave operator effectively pushes the current graphics state onto the graphics state stack, making it available later for **grestore**. The stack-based nature of the graphics state stack makes **gsave** and **grestore** nestable up to the limits of the graphics state stack, which is typically about 20 levels or more.

In the Display PostScript extensions to the PostScript language, the notion of a *graphics state object* has been introduced, which allows you to capture the current graphics state into an object that can be treated like any other object. There are companion operators like **setgstate** that will take a graphics state object and set all the current graphics state parameters according to its contents. This is much more flexible than the graphics state stack, since instantaneous changes can be made to the graphics state without having to push and pop the current state.

CONCLUDING THOUGHTS

This chapter provided you with a brief overview of data types and some examples of how operators use the operand stack. The stack and its various uses have been presented in some depth, yet there is a lot to learn about the stack, and you may not yet feel you fully understand it. The next chapter sets forth still more wisdom about the operand stack, to help you learn to trust and rely upon this important resource.

EXERCISES

1. What is left on the operand stack after the following code is executed?

```
/Times-Roman 24 selectfont
100 dup moveto
(Vocabulary) stringwidth 2 div neg rmoveto (Vocabulary) show
```

2. For each of the following code segments, determine what error, if any, would arise (not all of the code segments raise errors):

a. (string one) (string2) copy

b. 12 /Times-Roman findfont scalefont setfont

c. % center some text
```
306 500 moveto /Times-Bold 14 selectfont
(Report Title) dup stringwidth 2 div 0 rmoveto
show
```

d. save
```
    /Optima 12 selectfont 20 40 moveto
    (Save me!) dup show
restore
```

3. Rewrite the following code using just stack operators, without storing anything into a dictionary.

```
36 750 moveto /Times-Roman 24 selectfont
% works like "show", leaving current point at proper location
/ushow                    % linethickness lineposition (words) ushow -
{ %def
    LOCAL begin
        /text exch def
        /linepos exch def
        /linethick exch def
        gsave
            0 linepos rmoveto
            text stringwidth rlineto
            linethick setlinewidth stroke
        grestore
        text show
    end
} dup 0 4 dict put def
0.5 -4 (test underlined text) ushow
```

Chapter 6

Trusting the Stack

Most beginning PostScript programmers don't trust the operand stack. It seems like just a vehicle for transporting data to their procedures, and the sooner the data can be retrieved from the stack and put safely into a variable, the happier the programmer is.

There is a vague truth to this feeling, but it has only to do with the programmer, and not the PostScript language itself. It is a bit more difficult to think like a stack-based interpreter, so you can get confused about what is on the stack, how it got there, and what you should do with it, and this confusion can lead to bugs and lost data. However, since you cannot avoid the operand stack when writing PostScript programs, it is best just to master it, rather than to mistrust it.

SAFETY OF DATA ON THE STACK

In truth, the safest place for a piece of data is on the operand stack, with a few small caveats.

- If your program has bugs, you may inadvertently remove something from the operand stack that you needed, or leave something extra that will cause some later operation to trip over it. Sometimes these stack alignment programs persist for a long time, unless you consistently test all the paths through your program.

- Stack-based manipulations of more than a few operations or more than a few operands can be tricky to read and maintain, leading to the bugs just mentioned.

- If you transfer control temporarily to some other program, as you might do with an embedded illustration, for example, you should not be surprised if something you left on the operand stack is no longer there.

In general, the cleanest, fastest and best programs are those that make judicious use of the operand stack. As a rough rule of thumb, in designing a PostScript program you should spend 65 percent of your time thinking about the order of operands on the stack, whether or not you should divide all of your coordinate numbers by 1,000 before sending them to the interpreter, and whether you can get away without sending the X coordinate every time you plot a vertical line. You should spend 20 percent of your time adjusting the procedures you have defined to match the decisions you have made about operand order and use. (The remaining 15 percent is for debugging and getting distracted.)

Of course, these principles of careful use of the operand stack are derived primarily from printer drivers, which are inherently batch programs. If you are writing an interactive application in PostScript, or if you are writing a utility program that is entirely self-contained, you may have different goals—but the basic ideas still apply. The data must be on the operand stack in order for any PostScript operator to use it, so you might as well take advantage of that premise and try not to take things off the stack and put them on too many times unnecessarily.

The name of this chapter is the key: *trust* the operand stack. You should not simply follow a recipe that says always to use the stack or always to use variable names. Use the operand stack wisely, use it when speed is important, and use it because it is already there. Use it because you have mastered it and have learned its strengths and weaknesses and because you have to use it anyway.

Remember that the operand stack is used by every PostScript operator and procedure as the way to pass data and operands. The more cleanly your program supports this natural interface, the faster and more efficient it will be.

WHERE ARE THE DATA GOING?

One of the important things to consider when you're designing a PostScript program is what you're using the stack for at any given moment. Are you passing parameters to a function? Is the information on the stack raw data? Will the information be used once or many times? If you only need the data once, it is best to arrange it in such a way that you can use the data directly from the operand stack and never think about it again.

A common approach to dealing with data on the operand stack is to store the data under some name in a dictionary, rather than leaving the values on the operand stack. This has a few advantages.

- The data can be recalled onto the stack many times.
- Debugging can be easier with named data.
- Storing the data helps to minimize nasty stack manipulations.

The first few times you try to read or write PostScript programs, it may be difficult to understand what is going on in a statement like the one in Example 6.1. What is **exch** doing exactly where you would expect to see the value part of the definition?

As you know, the **def** operator requires its key and value in a particular order on the stack. If the *value*—the object you want to store—got put on the operand stack before you had a chance to put the *key*—the name under which you store that value—on the stack, then you would have them in the wrong order for **def**. In this case, you need to call **exch** to get them in the right order. It gets just slightly more confusing when the expression is buried inside a procedure somewhere. You can't see the value at all in that case, because it isn't on the stack yet. It won't be until you run the program and some operation produces the value as it executes.

If you call a procedure with many pieces of data on the operand stack as arguments, it can be a little bit tricky to get them stored into a dictionary. The typical trick is to associate keys with them and to execute **def**. A small amount of operand stack manipulation is required. Since the operands are in stack order, they need to be taken from the stack in the opposite order (see Example 6.1).

Example 6.1: Using *exch def* in a Procedure

```
/proc                        % A B C proc -
{ %def
        /C exch def
        /B exch def
        /A exch def
} def

(a) (b) (c) proc
```

Remember that the code fragment

```
(a) /A exch def
```

is equivalent to

```
/A (a) def
```

(without the **exch**), which is why it works. (See also Thinking Backward and Sideways in Chapter 5.)

Once you have collected the operands into the current dictionary, you simply call them by name in order to use them. Each time you supply the name in your program, it will be looked up in the current dictionary (or dictionary stack) and the value will be placed on the operand stack again.

REARRANGING THE STACK

If you want to use the operand stack directly in your program, the chances are you will need to perform some stack manipulation. It's almost unavoidable. There are a few operators that you will find indispensable for stack manipulation. There are also some techniques worth learning to help you keep bugs out of your stack exercises. Table 6.1 contains a summary of the stack operators in the PostScript language for quick reference. Don't worry if you don't understand how to use all the operators in the table; it will become more clear as you read on.

Table 6.1: PostScript Stack Manipulation Operators

Arguments	Operator	Action
| any_1 ... any_n	**clear**	discard all elements
mark obj_1 ... obj_n	**cleartomark**	discard everything through mark
A B C 3	**copy** B C A B C	duplicate top three elements
| any_1 ... any_n	**count** any_1 ... any_n n	count elements on stack
mark any_objects	**counttomark** mark any n	count elements down to mark
any	**dup** any any	duplicate top element
any_1 any_2	**exch** any_2 any_1	exchange top two elements
D E F G 2	**index** D E F G E	duplicate second element from top (where top is *0th* element)
	mark mark	push mark on stack
any	**pop**	discard top element
a b c d e f 3 -2	**roll** a b c f d e	take top three elements and roll negative two times

The most important operators for stack manipulation are **dup**, **exch**, **index**, and **roll**. Of these four operators, **dup** and **exch** are fairly easy to understand, since they apply only to the topmost item or items on the stack, but **index** and **roll** can be a bit more confusing.

Using the **dup** and **index** Operators

Although the **dup** operator is very simple in its operation, knowing when and how to use it effectively requires some skill in manipulating the operand stack. The **index** operator has almost exactly the same function as **dup**, except it will let you duplicate an object further down on the operand stack (**dup** duplicates only the topmost object). There are two or three places where these operators are used most commonly.

1. If you need to use a piece of data twice, use **dup** to make a temporary copy of the data. The copy will be used by the first operation, leaving the original data for the second operation.

2. When you are debugging, you can make a temporary copy of an object (using **dup**) to print or write to a debugging file without disturbing the execution of the program.

3. In a loop where you may need the same piece of data each time around the loop, that data can be left on the operand stack and it can be copied (with **dup** or **index**) each time before it is used inside the loop. Just make sure to remove it from the stack when you exit the loop. This technique can be seen in Example 6.2.

Example 6.2: Using *index* in a Loop Body

```
/Encoding 256 array def
Encoding               % leave on operand stack throughout loop
0 1 255 { %for
        1 index        % dup the Encoding array object on stack
        exch           % correct order for "put"
        /.notdef put
} bind for
pop                    % get rid of extra copy of Encoding
```

Using the **roll** Operator

The **roll** operator is one of the most useful stack operators, and one of the most confusing. Its purpose is to rearrange several of the topmost operands on the stack by rolling them. It takes two operands: one to supply the total number of elements to participate in the **roll** operation (this total is called the *roll group* in the following discussion) and the other to indicate how many elements within that total should actually be rolled (called the *roll amount*).

Let's look at the anatomy of the **roll** operator (Figure 6.1).

Figure 6.1: Anatomy of the *roll* Operator

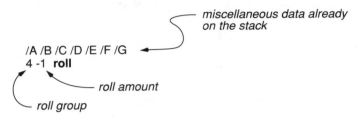

One helpful way to conceptualize the **roll** operator is to verbalize it. For the example shown in Figure 6.1, one might say "Take the top four elements on the stack and roll it negative one times." The top four elements are easy enough to understand, but what does it mean to roll something "negative one times?" The sign of the number (negative or positive) indicates the direction to roll, and the magnitude of the number indicates the number of elements to be rolled. The easiest way to think of the direction of the roll is like this:

- If the roll amount is negative, that means you take the elements from the bottom of the roll group and bring them to the top.
- If the roll amount is positive, you take the elements from the top of the stack and roll them to the bottom of the roll group.

Figure 6.2 and Figure 6.3 show the effects of rolling with a positive and a negative roll amount.

CONDITIONALS AND LOOPS

One of the most difficult things to do in PostScript programming is to make sure you don't inadvertently leave something on the stack or consume something from the stack that you weren't supposed to. Keeping track is easy enough when there is only a single path through the code, but if there are lots of **ifelse** statements and **loop** constructs, it gets more difficult to trace through all the possibilities to make sure you've not forgotten anything.

One of the most common instances of this problem is caused by operators that return different numbers of arguments depending on whether they succeed or fail. Example 6.3 shows a conditional that accidentally leaves a dictionary behind on the operand stack when the **where** operator succeeds (returns **true**), but works fine when the operator returns **false**.

Figure 6.2: Positive Rolling

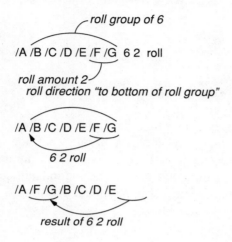

Figure 6.3: Negative Rolling

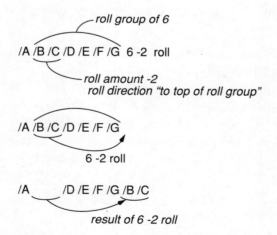

Example 6.3: Accidentally Leaving Dictionary on Stack

```
/selectfont where not { %if
      /selectfont { %def
            exch findfont exch scalefont
            setfont
      } def
} if
```

Unfortunately, the **where** operator returns the dictionary in which the key is found in the event that it does find the key, but returns nothing other than the boolean if it does not find the key. Example 6.4 shows a simple fix to correct this problem. The **if** statement is changed to **ifelse**, and the extra dictionary is popped from the stack if the **where** operator returns **true**.

Example 6.4: Correctly Maintaining Dictionary Stack

```
/selectfont where not { %if
      /selectfont { %def
            exch findfont exch scalefont
            setfont
      } def
}{ %else
      pop               % throw away dictionary returned by "where"
} ifelse
```

Table 6.2 provides a list of operators that can cause you some trouble by returning sometimes unexpected results on the operand stack. If you get a typecheck error that you have trouble finding, this might be the cause.

Table 6.2: Operators with Unexpected Stack Results

Operator	Results Returned
anchorsearch	different results on success and failure
for	unexpected loop index
forall	different results with different data types
scalefont	returns scaled dictionary onto stack
search	different results on success and failure
stringwidth	unexpected extra y value
where	different results on success and failure

RECURSION AND LOCAL VARIABLES

If you create a procedure that calls itself recursively, you have to be careful about the names you use. Recursion is inherently stack-based. To make recursion work correctly in PostScript, you need either to use the dictionary stack or the operand stack to store intermediate results until your recursion is unwound back to the original invocation level.

Let's look at a recursive function that has an integer passed to it as an argument, and that will ultimately return an integer as its result (Example 6.5). If the argument is even, the function calls itself recursively and adds one to the argument. If the argument is odd, the function returns. The result of this function is always an odd number.

Example 6.5: Recursion Using the Dictionary Stack

```
/recurse_proc              % int recurse_proc int
{ %def
      save
      2 dict begin
            /save_obj exch def
            /arg exch def
            arg 2 div truncate
            2 mul cvi
            arg eq { %ifelse
                  % even number
                  arg 1 add recurse_proc
            }{ %else
                  arg
            } ifelse
            save_obj        % leave on stack
      end
      restore               % to save_obj on stack
} bind def
2 recurse_proc
```

If you want to store the function's argument in a dictionary, you have to create a new dictionary and push it onto the dictionary stack each time the function is called, to maintain the name local to that instance of the function. In this example, the memory allocated by the dictionary is reclaimed by **save** and **restore**, putting each save object into the recursion dictionary until it is needed. If the function is called recursively, more than one save object may be generated, but each will ultimately be restored as the recursive calls return.

In Example 6.6 is the same procedure as the one in Example 6.5, rewritten to use the operand stack instead of the dictionary stack. This looks much simpler and better than using the dictionary stack, but if your recursive procedure requires more than a couple of operands, you may have a difficult time writing and understanding it if you use only the operand stack for your recursion. One additional advantage to this method is that it does not require memory allocation (for the local dictionary) or use of **save** and **restore**, and there are fewer instructions executed overall.

Example 6.6: Recursion Using the Operand Stack

```
/recurse_proc                 % int recurse_proc int
{ %def
        dup 2 div truncate
        2 mul cvi
        1 index eq { %ifelse
                % even number
                1 add recurse_proc
        } if
} bind def

2 recurse_proc
```

There are several ways to accomplish recursion, as you have seen. None of them is perfect, due partly to the lack of true local variables in the PostScript language. It is easy enough to implement recursion, though, and you need only exercise a reasonable amount of care to keep out of trouble and to avoid **execstackoverflow**, **dictstackoverflow**, or **stackoverflow** errors.

CONCLUDING THOUGHTS

The operand stack is an integral part of the PostScript language, and you cannot avoid using it. Once you start to understand it and to trust it, you will be able to write programs that make very effective use of the stack. A stack-based language seems to make you think backward and upside-down, but in fact it only makes you think in chunks, where each chunk is the result of one operation. Every operator is grouped with its operands, and the program is almost read from the middle outward, rather than from top to bottom or from bottom to top.

This chapter touched upon the use of conditionals and loops; the next two chapters address these in much greater detail.

EXERCISES

1. What is the result of the following short piece of PostScript code?

   ```
   0 0 10 100 { add } for
   ```

2. What are the contents of the operand stack after executing the following program segment?

   ```
   clear
   /A /B /C /D /E /a /b /c /d /e
   2 copy 6 index 6 index 12 -4 roll exch 5 3 roll
   ```

3. Write a procedure called **reversestack** that will reverse the contents of the operand stack (the topmost element becomes the bottom element).

4. Write a procedure called **standardfonts** that finds all fonts defined in **FontDirectory** that have a standard encoding. You can assume the presence of the built-in name **StandardEncoding** and use it to compare to the **Encoding** in each font. This procedure should not define any variables. Leave the names of the fonts on the operand stack.

Chapter 7

Building Conditional Statements

A conditional is what most people call an **if** statement. It provides a mechanism for executing one piece of code or another based on a condition that is evaluated while the program is running. In the PostScript language, there are two operators for building conditional statements: **if** and **ifelse**. The only difference between them is that the **if** statement has only one clause and the **ifelse** statement has two. There is no built-in **case** statement in the PostScript language, but in this chapter we will discuss how to fabricate one.

Conditionals are the most fundamental and most useful construction in any programming language. A conditional belongs to a family of notions known as *control structures*, which are program mechanisms for letting you execute different parts of a program discontinuously, rather than having the whole program be one long piece of string. Other control structures are **while** loops, **case** statements, **goto** instructions, and subroutines. The ability to *branch* to a different part of your program when certain conditions are met is absolutely crucial to any moderately complex program. You should learn inside and out how **if** and **ifelse** work in the PostScript language.

SIMPLE CONDITIONALS

The simplest way to build a conditional statement in your program is to use the template technique, as in Example 7.1.

Example 7.1: Constructing a Conditional

```
% the conditional expression comes first
myvariable 3 gt { %ifelse

}{ %else

} ifelse
```

This creates an empty conditional statement with the conditional expression in place. The **if** and **else** clauses can then be filled in after the template is in place as shown in Example 7.2. (For more information, refer back to Setting up Templates in Chapter 3.)

Example 7.2: Filling in the Conditional Template

```
/myvariable 0 def
myvariable 3 gt { %ifelse
        (my variable got to 3; resetting to 0) == flush
        /myvariable 0 store
}{ %else
        /myvariable myvariable 1 add store
        (my variable is now ) print
        myvariable == flush
} ifelse
```

A standard way of thinking about a conditional statement is to state the expression out loud, and to imagine first the **true** clause, then the **false** clause. That is the way the **ifelse** statement is laid out in the PostScript language. You have to remember that the **ifelse** operator itself goes at the end of the construction (as in the examples given). But you can still think of the conditional in much the same way you think in any other programming language (Example 7.3).

Example 7.3: Thinking through a Conditional

```
% if the variable is greater than three,
myvariable 3 gt { %ifelse
        % then set it back to 0,
        /myvariable 0 def
}{ %else
        %otherwise, add one to it and tell me its current value:
        /myvariable myvariable 1 add store
        (my variable is now ) print
        myvariable == flush
} ifelse
```

As long as you think about your algorithm as a straightforward sequence of steps and can figure out how to write the expression and each of the clauses, the **ifelse** statement itself should be easy to master. You can lay it out in a template in seconds. Then you are left with the task of the carefully implementing the algorithm, not the details of the conditional statement.

The major advantage to the indentation style and position of the **{ }** braces seen in these examples is that program lines can be easily added to or deleted from the clauses of the **ifelse** statement without disrupting the syntactic balance of the braces. This becomes especially important when braces are nested several deep.

SETTING UP THE CONDITION

All conditional statements depend on something being true or false. There are many PostScript operators that return a boolean value (remember, this just means that it can only be **true** or **false**). The purpose of this boolean returned on the operand stack is so that you can use it with an **ifelse** statement. The simplest of these is the **eq** operator (see Example 7.4).

Example 7.4: Setting Up the Conditional

```
dup type /stringtype eq { %ifelse
        % topmost element on stack is a string
}{ %else
        % it is not a string
} ifelse
```

Remember that comparing an object to another object with **eq** pops both objects from the stack before pushing the result of the comparison. If you need the object again, you should either use **dup** to make a copy before you compare, or give the object a name in a dictionary (see Declaring and Using Variables in Chapter 3).

There are many other operators that return booleans. For example, the **readhexstring** operator returns a boolean, even though most of the examples of its use (with the **image** operator, especially) simply throw the boolean away. For a more careful use of this boolean, see Example 7.5.

Example 7.5: Using a Conditional with *readhexstring*

```
currentfile 128 string readhexstring { %ifelse
        % readhexstring filled up the buffer
}{ %else
        % it encountered EOF or other problems
} ifelse
```

Table 7.1 shows the most useful PostScript operators that return booleans. An **ifelse** or **if** statement can follow any of these operators. In fact, the operators were designed to be followed by a conditional.

Table 7.1: PostScript Operators that Return Boolean Values

Arguments	Operator	Action
any_1 any_2	**eq** *bool*	test equal to
any_1 any_2	**ne** *bool*	test not equal to
obj_1 obj_2	**ge** *bool*	test greater than or equal to
obj_1 obj_2	**gt** *bool*	test greater than
obj_1 obj_2	**le** *bool*	test less than or equal to
obj_1 obj_2	**lt** *bool*	test less than
$bool_1$ $bool_2$	**and** $bool_3$	logical and
$bool_1$	**not** $bool_2$	logical not
$bool_1$ $bool_2$	**or** $bool_3$	logical inclusive or
$bool_1$ $bool_2$	**xor** $bool_3$	logical exclusive or
	true *true*	push boolean value true
	false *false*	push boolean value false
dict key	**known** *bool*	test whether key is in *dict*
key	**where** *dict true*	find *dict* in which *key* is defined
	false	

string seek	**anchorsearch**	post match true	determine if *seek* is initial substring of *string*
	or	string false	or return *string* if not
string seek	**search**	post match pre true	search for *seek* in *string*
	or	string false	
string	**token**	post token true false	read a token from start of *string*
any	**stopped**	bool	execute and catch any call to **stop**
any	**xcheck**	bool	test executable attribute
string	**rcheck**	bool	test read access
string	**wcheck**	bool	test write access
file_object	**read**	int true false	read one character from file
file_object string	**readhexstring**	substring boolean	read string in hexadecimal from *file_object* into buffer *string*
file_object string	**readline**	string bool	read through newline
file_object	**token**	token true false	read PostScript token from file
file_object	**status**†	boolean	is *file_object* still valid?

NOTE: Operators marked by a dagger (†) are not available in all interpreters; check before executing.

It is also useful to combine a few simple operations into powerful tests. In Example 7.6 are some techniques for type checking and other tasks, in the context of other simple procedures.

The program in Example 7.7 will open up a file from the disk and print (or display) it one line at a time, starting a new page as necessary. There are several interesting conditionals here, based on the current point and the results of the **readline** operator.

Example 7.6: Procedure with Typechecking

```
/typecheck_moveto { %def
        % if either argument is not a number, use 0
        dup type /realtype ne
        1 index type /integertype ne or { %if
                pop 0
        } if
        exch
        dup type /realtype ne
        1 index type /integertype ne or { %if
                pop 0
        } if
        exch moveto
} bind def
```


Example 7.7: Conditionals at Work

```
% note: this program will only work on a UNIX workstation, since it explicitly
% opens the file /etc/passwd and uses the non-standard "selectfont" operator
/bottom 72 def
/lineshow                    % (string) lineshow -
{ %def
        % works like show, but checks for bottom
        % of page and also moves current point
        % down one line after each call
        currentpoint exch pop% just the Y coord
        bottom lt { %if
                showpage
                72 750 moveto% top of new page
        } if
        gsave show grestore
        0 -12 rmoveto        % down one line
} bind def

%list the /etc/passwd file
/Times-Roman 10 selectfont
72 750 moveto
/datafile (/etc/passwd) (r) file def
/buffer 256 string def
```

```
{ %loop
        datafile buffer readline { %ifelse
                lineshow
        }{ %else
                fd closefile showpage exit
        } ifelse
} bind loop
```

A very common source of program bugs is to have one **else** clause in a conditional that leaves something on the operand stack (or uses too many elements from it). If you change the conditional expression so that the stack holds different elements, be careful to debug each of the individual clauses fully. If the **else** clauses handle obscure possibilities or error conditions, they may not be executed (and hence debugged) under normal testing, but may fail under heavy use. Watch for this source of errors and bugs, and try to develop a sound methodology that will help to eliminate the cause of them.

TIP

It is important to test both the **true** and **false** clauses of your conditional statements, especially as you gradually change your code and evolve the contents or the type of items on the stack before going into the conditional. You can "rig" this testing by redefining the **ifelse** operator to reverse the sense of all your conditionals (see Example 7.8), just to give a dry run through them, or you can test each one by hand.

Example 7.8: Redefining *ifelse* for Testing

```
% flip the sense of "ifelse" so you can test both sides of the operation
/orig_ifelse /ifelse load def
/ifelse                         % boolean { true_proc } { false_proc } ifelse
{
        exch            % execute procs in other order
        orig_ifelse
} bind def
```

As you gain more experience with the language, you will become expert in the use of the **ifelse** statement, which is a fundamental and useful operator in any PostScript language program.

CONDITIONALS ARE NOT MAGIC

A conditional statement is not magic. There is no operator in the PostScript language that is different from the others. Even though you will learn to think of the entire conditional as a single construction, it is not. Only the execution of the **if** and **ifelse** operators make something into a conditional. Otherwise, and until you execute one of those operators, the rest of the code is just a couple of procedures and a boolean on the operand stack.

Just to confuse you and to reinforce this point, let's look at a simple conditional rearranged in a perfectly legal, although somewhat unusual, configuration. The first conditional (Example 7.9) is very straightforward. The second program (Example 7.10) has the same result, but is constructed very differently. The procedures for the **true** and **false** clauses are defined like any other procedure, then brought up on the operand with the **load** operator, ready for the final execution of **ifelse**. As an added twist, a random string is put on the stack in between, and then moved out of the way.

Example 7.9: Basic Conditional Statement

```
currentpoint exch pop 72 le { %ifelse
        showpage 72 650 moveto
}{
        0 -12 rmoveto
} ifelse
```

Example 7.10: The Same Conditional Built on the Fly

```
% set up procedures to generate a boolean and to act as the
% "true" and "false" procedure bodies for "ifelse"
/off_bottom_of_page          % off_bottom_of_page bool
{ %def
        currentpoint exch pop 72 le         % boolean is on stack
} bind def
/off_bottom_proc { showpage 72 650 moveto } bind def
/regular_proc { 0 -12 rmoveto } bind def

% now invoke the conditional by loading the boolean and
% the two procedures onto the stack and rearranging them a
% little bit to show there is no magic:
```

```
off_bottom_of_page              % boolean
/regular_proc load              % "false" proc
(a random string)
/off_bottom_proc load           % "true" proc
exch pop exch                   % get rid of random string
ifelse
```

Another interesting example that illustrates the fact that **ifelse** is just an ordinary operator is Example 7.11, which redefines the **ifelse** operator to get a little extra information while it is executing, for debugging purposes.

Example 7.11: Redefining *ifelse* for Debugging

```
% redefine "ifelse" to trace which clause is being executed:
/orig_ifelse /ifelse load def
/ifelse                         % bool proc₁ proc₂ ifelse
{ %def
        2 index dup             % look at the boolean
        (condition: ) print ==
        { %ifelse               % show us which proc will execute
            1 index ==          % show the "true" procedure
        }{ %else
            dup ==              % show the "false" procedure
        } orig_ifelse
        orig_ifelse             % now execute "ifelse" normally
} bind def
```

NESTED CONDITIONALS AND **ELSE** CLAUSES

Fairly often, in a complicated program, you need to have conditionals that have more conditionals on each of the two result clauses. When these nest more than one level deep, it can become tricky to maintain them without leaving things on the operand stack or introducing bugs of some sort.

The first issue is simply balancing the curly braces correctly, so that there are no basic syntactic errors in the program. Using the template technique for this is a good approach, and one that can be expanded as necessary later (see Example 7.12).

Example 7.12: Nested Conditionals

```
myfont /Optima eq { %ifelse
        ptsize 12 eq { %ifelse
        }{ %else
                ptsize 100 gt { %ifelse
                }{ % else
                } ifelse
        } ifelse
}{ % else
} ifelse
```

The second important thing to keep straight in a complicated nested conditional statement is the contents of the operand stack. This is particularly important if you use **dup** or keep data on the operand stack that must survive into the middle of the conditional somewhere. Otherwise, nested conditionals are fairly straightforward to use.

TIP   If you use **ifelse** rather than **if**, make sure you supply both procedures, and that you think carefully about what is on the operand stack for each of them.

COMPOUND CONDITIONALS

Compound conditionals are found wherever there is a single condition but many possible **else** clauses. In other languages, this might be handled by a **case** statement, but—as you've already learned—there is no **case** operator in the PostScript language.

First, let's look at an example of a compound conditional implemented in the most straightforward manner, as a series of **else** clauses. Remember that PostScript is not a compiled language. Therefore, you should try to put the most likely conditions first, since they will be tested in order. Since there is no way to choose from a parallel set of procedure bodies, the only way to implement a compound conditional with **ifelse** is to nest the conditionals, adding a new test for each **else** clause. This can get very tricky to maintain, since it may nest very deep to supply all of the required clauses (see Example 7.13).

You can imagine how complicated that would get if you had twenty or thirty different commands to look for. Example 7.14 uses a very slightly different structure for the same conditional that makes it a little flatter and easier to maintain.

Example 7.13: Compound Conditional with *ifelse*

```
% read a token from the input stream and look for a command
% like "PRINT", "QUIT", or "HELP".

currentfile 256 string readline token { %ifelse
        % a token is a command
        dup /PRINT eq { %ifelse
                do_print
        }{ %else
                dup /QUIT eq { %ifelse
                        do_quit
                }{ %else
                        dup /HELP eq { %ifelse
                                do_help
                        }{ %else
                                do_unknown
                        } ifelse
                } ifelse
        } ifelse
}{ %else
        (no more commands.) =
        stop
} ifelse
```

Example 7.14: Compound Conditional with *loop*

```
currentfile 256 string readline token { %ifelse
        % a token is a command
        { %dummy loop, always exited
                dup /PRINT eq { do_print exit } if
                dup /QUIT eq { do_quit exit } if
                dup /HELP eq { do_help exit } if
                do_unknown
                exit
        } loop
}{ %else
        (no more commands.) = stop
} ifelse
```

Example 7.15 presents one more way to set up a compound conditional, one that uses the power and flexibility of the PostScript language, particularly the name lookup and dictionary mechanisms. In this implementation, the multiple cases are stored as procedures in a dictionary (the current dictionary, for simplicity in this example), and the command string is looked up in the current dictionary and executed. Note that this requires only a single conditional (for the unknown case).

Example 7.15: Compound Conditional Using Name Lookup

```
/commands 4 dict def
commands begin
/PRINT { do_print } def
/QUIT { do_quit } def
/HELP { do_help } def
currentfile 256 string readline token { %ifelse
        % a token is a command
        dup where { %ifelse
                exch get exec
        }{ %else
                do_unknown
        } ifelse
}{ %else
        (no more commands.) = stop
        end % commands dictionary
} ifelse
```

As you can see, there are several approaches to setting up a compound conditional. The language is very flexible, but it is a bit of trouble to do without a **case** statement.

CONCLUDING THOUGHTS

The most important thing to remember about conditionals and the **ifelse** operator is that the whole construction is interpreted each time it is encountered. The condition (**true** or **false**) is computed each time, the two procedure bodies are loaded onto the operand stack, and the **ifelse** operator pushes one or the other of them onto the operand stack. There's nothing really magical about the way it works, and the procedure bodies it uses are interchangeable with all other procedures in the PostScript language.

The next chapter presents a look at looping constructs. Loops share many properties with conditionals, since they require procedure bodies as arguments. Some of the concepts learned in this chapter will also apply in the next chapter.

EXERCISES

1. Design a **case** operator for the PostScript language, and design a procedure that will implement it. Think about the design trade-offs between ease of use (once your **case** operator exists) versus ease of implementation for you. Supply some simple documentation (comments in your program are good enough) explaining how to use your new **case** operator.

2. The following procedure emulates the **setcmykcolor** language extension by using **setrgbcolor** and doing a simple conversion. Design a conditional statement with the **where** operator that will define this procedure *only* if the **setcmykcolor** operator does not already exist.

```
/setcmykcolor { %def
    1 sub 4 1 roll
    3 { %repeat
        3 index add neg dup 0 lt {pop 0} if 3 1 roll
    } repeat setrgbcolor pop
} bind def
```

3. The "standard" procedure used with the **image** operator uses the **readhexstring** operator to get a line of data from the input file. The trouble is, it *ignores* the boolean returned by **readhexstring**, which is not really a good idea. Please rewrite this procedure body to check for the end-of-file condition reported by the **readhexstring** operator. (The second line of hex data is incomplete in this example, causing an error in the execution of the program as it stands. Fill out the line of data to see what the program is supposed to do.)

```
/picstr 16 string def
100 100 translate 100 900 scale
16 2 8 [ 16 0 0 16 0 0 ]
{ currentfile picstr readhexstring pop } image
00FF00FF00FF00FF00FF00FF00FF00FF
00FF00FF00FF00FF
```

Chapter 8

Using Looping Constructs

Loops are useful for repeating a sequence of steps in a quantized manner. There are various conditions under which looping is appropriate. One of the most common is to iterate over data structures of known size, such as arrays. Another use is to repeat a set of commands more than once.

If you want to perform a repetitive task that uses some fixed parameters, you generally think of loops in most programming languages. For example, you could create a grid of lines or a spiral of text by setting up a **for** loop and using the loop increment to set up the next line or the next rotation of characters.

One fairly common use of loops is to generate "synthetic" graphics. The data for a grid of lines or a spiral actually can be manufactured within the loop rather than being supplied as a large body of individual x, y coordinates and sequences of **moveto** and **lineto** instructions. However, using one of the loop operators can be an extremely useful technique even with real data that are not synthetically generated within the loop itself (as you'll see later in this chapter). For example, a routine to draw a polygon with hundreds of sides could benefit from being put into a loop.

LOOP BASICS

There are several different looping operators in the PostScript language (see Table 8.1). Each of them has a particular purpose and a style of use that is worth considering.

Table 8.1: Looping Operators

Arguments	Operator	Action
–	**exit** –	jump out of loop body immediately
pattern proc buffer	**filenameforall**	execute proc for each file that matches pattern string
start index end proc	**for** –	execute proc as many times as (end-start) / index dictates.
composite_obj proc	**forall** –	execute proc for each element of composite_obj
proc	**loop** –	execute proc indefinitely
count proc	**repeat**	execute proc exactly count times

If you want to execute a sequence of instructions a precise number of times, you should use either the **repeat** operator or the **for** operator. Use **repeat** if you don't need to use the loop index within the body of the loop (as discussed in the next section). If you want to keep executing a loop until some condition is met, you should use the **loop** operator, and use **exit** to pop out of the loop when the condition is satisfied. If you want to execute some instructions on each element of an array, a string, or a dictionary, you can use the **forall** operator, which supplies each element of a composite object to the loop as it is executing. This is useful for searching through arrays and sometimes for processing each character in a string, although it is a fairly labor-intensive operation compared to other string operators.

To construct a simple program loop, first start with a template for the loop body and make sure to supply the correct arguments for the looping operator you have chosen. Example 8.1 shows a simple **repeat** loop that draws an octagon; its result is displayed in Figure 8.1.

Example 8.1: Simple Loop to Draw an Octagon

```
4 setlinewidth
300 200 moveto
7 { %repeat
        0 100 rlineto
        45 rotate
} bind repeat
closepath stroke
```

Figure 8.1: Output of Example 8.1

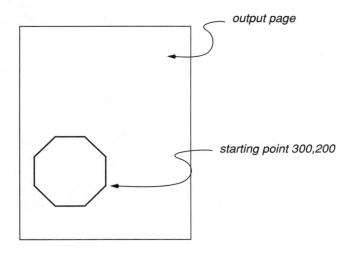

output page

starting point 300,200

USING THE LOOP INDEX

Looping operators are useful because they let a task be performed more than once. They can be even more useful when you keep track of the loop index and use it effectively.

Example 8.2: Ignoring Loop Index

```
gsave
        250 250 translate
        0 10 360 { %for
                pop                     % do not use loop index this time
                0 -50 moveto 200 0 lineto 0 50 lineto
                10 rotate
        } for
        stroke
grestore
```

Example 8.2 sets up the loop index to give 10-degree increments around a circle, but actually does not use the loop index explicitly within the loop. The results are shown in Figure 8.2.

Figure 8.2:Output of Example 8.2

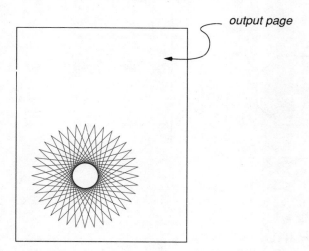

output page

In Example 8.3 is a short program that uses the loop index to set the line weight of a series of stroked lines and to control their spacing; its results are shown in Figure 8.3.

Example 8.3: Using Loop Index for Line Weight

```
00 100 translate
2 3 div setgray 0 0 612 250 rectfill
0 setgray
2 2 20 { %for
        dup setlinewidth      % use loop index as line weight
        0 exch 12 mul moveto% and use for line spacing
        612 0 rlineto
        stroke                    % must stroke to use line weight
} for
```

Figure 8.3: Output of Example 8.3

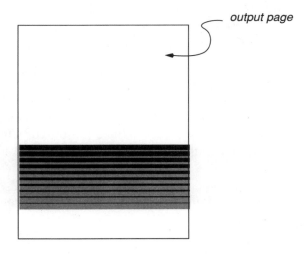

When using a loop index, make sure you either pop the unwanted data off the stack or use it within the loop body, or you will leave unwanted data on the operand stack which may affect other portions of the program.

Several looping operators push data onto the stack each time around the loop. In particular, the **forall** operator pushes each element of an array or string onto the stack; it pushes both the key and value for each dictionary entry onto the stack. Table 8.2 provides a summary of each looping operator and the data that are pushed onto the stack for each iteration of the loop.

Don't forget that the **for**, **forall**, **kshow**, and **filenameforall** looping operators push values onto the operand stack that must either be used or popped from the stack.

Table 8.2: Arguments Supplied by Looping Operators

Operator	Data Pushed onto Operand Stack for Each Iteration
for	loop index (integer)
forall	for strings: integer ASCII code for each byte of string for arrays: each element of the array, of arbitrary type for dictionaries: both the key and the value for each entry
kshow	character code for character just printed and for the character about to be printed
loop	none
repeat	none
filenameforall	a string containing each file name that matches the pattern

Example 8.4 shows both a **forall** loop and a **filenameforall** loop being used to find out all the font names defined in **FontDirectory** and on the disk of a printer. Notice the way that the data are used inside the loop bodies.

Example 8.4: Finding Font Names with Looping Operators

```
/scratch 128 string def
FontDirectory { %forall
        pop             % get rid of "value" part of dictionary entry
        scratch cvs print (\n) print
} bind forall
(fonts/*) { %filenameforall
        dup length 6 sub 6 exch getinterval print (\n) print
} scratch filenameforall
```

As you can see, there are a lot of ways to use the looping operators effectively, especially if you take advantage of the operators that push data onto the operand stack during execution of the loop body.

LOOPS ARE PROCEDURE BODIES

Since the *proc* passed to all of the looping operators is just an ordinary procedure body, you can perform any of the standard operations on it. One often-overlooked but very important detail is to apply **bind** to the procedure body before executing the loop instruction, so that the loop will execute more quickly (see Example 8.5). Be careful, however, not to apply **bind** to a loop that is inside a procedure body that has also been bound; it doesn't accomplish anything further (since **bind** applies to all nested procedure bodies recursively) and may degrade performance slightly if **bind** is executed each time the procedure is called.

Example 8.5: Using *bind* on Loop Bodies

```
0 1 1000 { %for
        0 moveto 0 400 rlineto stroke
} bind for
```

You can also take advantage of the fact that a loop body is an array (all procedures are arrays) and actually **put** objects directly into it to save time. Example 8.6 shows this technique applied to creating an **Encoding** array for a font, where you have to supply the array object itself 255 times during the execution of the loop. This saves the interpreter name lookup overhead each time around the loop.

Example 8.6: Putting Objects into Loop Bodies

```
/encoding currentfont /Encoding get def
0 1 255 { %for
        ENCODING_HERE exch /.notdef put
} dup 0 encoding put bind for
```

This example is a bit tricky, but it has a simple underlying concept. The trick is to put a dummy object into the procedure body (in this case, the executable name **ENCODING_HERE**, but it could be any object), then, before the procedure is ever executed, to replace that dummy object with the actual encoding array itself, instead of a name. The advantage to this approach is that you don't have to look up the name all 256 times around the loop; the array object itself is in the procedure body, which saves you 256 name lookups and a lot of time.

Even though **image**, **colorimage** and **imagemask** are not technically considered looping operators, they may in fact be executed many, many times. This makes them qualify as looping operators to a large degree, and the techniques just discussed also apply to these operators.

In the most standard situation where you supply the image data in-line in your input file and read from **currentfile**, the size of the buffer for **readhexstring** is typically only as big as one scan line of the image. This means that the data acquisition procedure for **image** or **imagemask** will be executed once for each scan line in the image, which may result in the procedure's being executed hundreds of times—that certainly qualifies it as a looping operation.

The technique just illustrated in Example 8.5 of using **bind** on the procedure body is a very good idea for images, and the idea presented in Example 8.6 can also be applied to both **currentfile** and the string buffer for **readhexstring**, as shown in Example 8.7. However, a slightly different approach will be used to construct the **image** procedure (other than using **put**), to make it a little bit more readable.

Example 8.7: Optimizing the Image Procedure

```
/currfile currentfile def          %get the current file object
/buffer 128 string def             % image buffer
128 400 1 [ 1 0 0 -1 0 400 ]
[ currentfile buffer /readhexstring cvx /pop cvx ] cvx bind
image
% hex data goes here
```

The procedure in this call to **image** now contains four objects, none of which are executable names, thanks to **bind** and the way we constructed the procedure. (The procedure contains a file object, a string object, and two operator objects.)

If you're having difficulty following the way the procedure body was constructed in Example 8.7, you might skip ahead and read Constructing an Array in Chapter 11.

LOOPS OF INSTRUCTIONS

One very powerful use of looping operators is to perform repeated instructions, such as a series of **lineto** or **curveto** operators. This can be particularly effective in a printer driver or any situation in which you might want to avoid repeating the names of the operators many times. Example 8.8 has a large number of repetitive instructions; the program sets several lines of text sequentially down the page. It can be written to minimize the number of individual instructions issued, as seen in Example 8.9.

Example 8.8: A Program with Repeated Instructions

```
72 750 moveto
/Times-Roman findfont 10 scalefont setfont
gsave
(Sometimes you have to construct a loop that may run for an indeterminate) show
grestore
0 -12 rmoveto
gsave
(length of time. For example, you might loop until an EOF condition is) show
grestore
0 -12 rmoveto
gsave
(met, or until no more spaces are found in a string, etc.) show
grestore
0 -12 rmoveto
```

Example 8.9: Using *repeat* for Instructions

```
72 750 moveto
/Times-Roman findfont 10 scalefont setfont
(met, or until no more spaces are found in a string, etc.)
(length of time. For example, you might loop until an EOF condition is)
(Sometimes you have to construct a loop that may run for an indeterminate)
3 { %repeat
        gsave show grestore 0 -12 rmoveto
} bind repeat
```

Figure 8.4: Output of Example 8.9

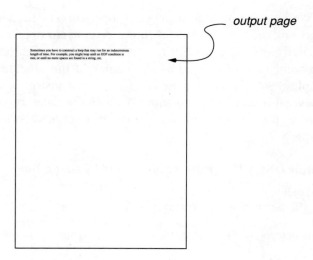

output page

EXITING LOOPS PREMATURELY

Sometimes you have to construct a loop that may run for an indeterminate amount of time. For example, you might loop until an end-of-file condition is met, or until no more spaces are found in a string. The best way to construct a loop of this type is to use the **loop** and **exit** operators. The **exit** operator will simply cause the innermost looping context to be broken, allowing exit from the loop at any point.

Here is the basic loop construct:

```
{ %loop
        exit_condition { exit } if
} loop
```

The *exit_condition* is some test that decides whether or not it is time to exit the loop. For example, in the program in Example 8.10, the exit condition is provided by the **readline** operator, which returns **false** if the end of the file is reached, **true** otherwise.

Example 8.10: Exiting a Loop

```
/fd (/user/glenn/Book/current/pictures/test.eps) (r) file def
/buff 128 string def
/Helvetica 10 selectfont
20 130 moveto
{ %loop
        fd buff readline { %else
                gsave show grestore
                0 -12 rmoveto
        } { fd closefile exit } ifelse
} bind loop
```

CONCLUDING THOUGHTS

In this chapter you have seen many different situations for loops, some of which use data, some of which use instructions, and some of which are simply executed until it is determined that they are done. It is up to you to decide which of the looping operators is best suited for your needs, and to use it appropriately. In the next chapter you will see how to construct and use procedures in your programs.

EXERCISES

1. Rewrite the following C program segment in PostScript.

```
main ()
{
    long factorial;
    int index;
    factorial = 1;
    for ( index = 10; index > 0; index-- )
    {
        factorial = factorial * index;
    }
    printf ( "10 factorial is %d\n", factorial );
}
```

2. Rewrite the following PostScript code fragment using a **repeat** loop. Don't worry about manufacturing the data inside the loop, just use the data directly from the operand stack.

```
0 0 moveto
100 200 lineto
200 200 lineto
300 400 lineto
400 400 lineto
500 600 lineto
600 600 lineto
closepath fill
```

3. Write a loop that takes a single string on the operand stack, counts the number of spaces in the string, and returns the string and an integer count of spaces back on the operand stack when finished. For this exercise, use the **search**, **loop**, and **exit** operators.

4. Rewrite the above exercise using the **forall** operator instead of **search** and **loop**.

5. Find the bugs in the following program (there are at least two or three of them). The program should print a grid of 20 lines by 10 lines.

```
% draw a grid of 20 x 10 lines
save
    0.1 setlinewidth
    20 20 translate
    0 10 200 { %for
        dup 0 moveto 0 100 rlineto
    } for
    stroke
    0 10 100 { %for
        0 1 index moveto 200 0 rlineto
    } for
    stroke
restore
```

Chapter 9

Procedures

In most programming languages, *procedures* are used to group together a set of instructions into a package that can be given a name and invoked by that name. The PostScript language provides a similar mechanism, although it is not as formal as many other languages. In particular, there are no local variables or specific parameter-passing conventions. It is up to you to decide what resources the procedure will use and how it will interact with its environment.

A PostScript procedure does not have to take its "traditional" form as a parcel of instructions to be called as a sort of subroutine. In fact, procedure bodies are used in many places without having names at all. For example, an **ifelse** statement requires two procedure bodies among its arguments, although only one of them is used each time **ifelse** is invoked.

In traditional procedural programming languages, a distinction is made between a procedure and a *function*. A function is simply a set of instructions that returns a value or values to the caller. For example, if you wanted to compute the average of three numbers, you might use a function that had three operands passed to it and returned a real number (their average). In most traditional procedural programming languages, you need to specify what kind of value will be returned by the function while you are setting up the function itself.

PostScript procedures can act as functions quite simply by leaving something behind on the operand stack when they exit. In fact, since there is no compile-time checking of your program, a procedure might return a value inadvertently. Furthermore, a PostScript procedure acting as a function can return a value of any type, which is both good and bad. Although there are explicit data types in the PostScript language, the lack of a compile cycle forces run-time type checking, which, although it does a good job of checking types, often does so a bit too late.

WHAT EXACTLY IS A PROCEDURE?

In formal PostScript language terms, a *procedure body* is just an executable array, which is an array of PostScript objects that has its executable flag set. There are no further requirements of a procedure from the language's point of view. In fact, the procedure does not even have to be composed of legal language elements for you to declare it. Since PostScript is an interpreted language, it is not until you try to run the program that the procedure will be interpreted (and that you will find out if it is written reasonably).

There are several places where procedure bodies are often found (or are required).

- Procedure bodies are used with operators like **loop**, **for**, **forall**, and **filenameforall**.
- Procedure bodies are used in **ifelse** statements to provide the **true** and **false** clauses of the conditional.
- Some operators—including **image**, **kshow**, **forall**, **settransfer**, and others related to these—require procedure bodies as operands.
- User-defined procedures can behave just like built-in operators, and are a useful way to extend the language.

Let's look at a typical procedure definition and its use (Example 9.1).

Example 9.1: Typical Procedure Definition

```
/S { moveto show } def
(some text) 100 200 S
```

The procedure's name is **S**, and it takes three bits of data as parameters: two real numbers (the *x* and *y* locations for **moveto**) and a string.

There is no mention of parameters or data required on the operand stack in the typical procedure definition. It's okay to define procedures that are dependent on the operand stack, because you have to use them, and only you must keep the contents of the stack straight. The language does not enforce it, other than by generating an error if something doesn't work.

In order to gain a real understanding of this common procedure definition and invocation, let's rearrange it in some interesting ways, all of which are legal and will work just fine. Example 9.2 sets forth some alternative ways to define the **S** procedure of Example 9.1.

Example 9.2: Alternative Ways to Define a Procedure

```
(S) cvn { moveto show } def

{ moveto show } /S exch def

currentdict /S { moveto show } put

/S [ (moveto) cvn (show) cvn ] cvx def
```

All of the definitions shown in Example 9.2 have exactly the same effect. They are not different procedure definitions, they are the same procedure definition, accomplished in various ways. This illustrates that procedures are not magic; they are simply a collection of instructions in an executable array.

You can associate a procedure body with a name if you like, by creating a definition in a dictionary. This can be done in various ways (including use of **put** as shown as the third alternative in Example 9.2), but the simplest of them is the method that just uses the **def** operator. The **def** operator is very simplistic. All it does is take two objects and make an association between them in the current dictionary. It does not help you write correct programs. In particular, you don't have to use a name as the key, and if you get things backwards, it won't complain.

```
{ moveto show } /S def
```

In this case, of course, if you tried to use the **S** procedure, it would tell you it was **undefined**, because it has no dictionary entry with **S** as the key. Now let's look at the procedure call itself, which requires three values to be on the operand stack.

```
(some text) 100 200 S
```

This can be looked at as a single procedure call and its arguments, although it is better to keep in mind that the interpreter does not see it that way. It sees simply a sequence of tokens to execute.

```
(some text)
100
200
S
```

Of course, the string (**some text**) and the numbers **100** and **200** are literal objects, so they are simply pushed onto the operand stack. When the **S** is encountered, looked up, and the procedure is executed, the correct arguments just happen to be on the operand stack.

PARAMETER PASSING

The best way to pass specific information to a procedure is to place it on the operand stack. There is, however, no procedure declaration to give names to the parameters. In fact, no rule says you must use the parameters. The cooperation between the definition of the procedure and its invocation is entirely up to you. In general, though, a procedure should consume all of its operands from the stack, unless it returns a value of some kind.

Example 9.3: Procedure *S* of Example 9.1

```
/S { moveto show } def
(some text) 100 200 S
```

The procedure **S** in Example 9.3 has three parameters, a string body and the *x*, *y* coordinates. These are supplied on the operand stack in the order required. That is, since **moveto** must be executed before **show**, the parameters used by **moveto** appear on the top of the stack. Note that this requires them to be actually written after the string, so that they will be on top (last in, first out). Let's rearrange this example a little to see what is going on (Example 9.4).

Example 9.4: Procedure *S* and Data Rearranged

```
(some text) 100 200 /S { moveto show } def S
```

This also is perfectly legal. The procedure is defined just before it is invoked, with the operands delicately hanging on the operand stack. This probably is not the way you would write a program like this, but it makes it a little easier to imagine how the procedure evolved, and to see how the operands are used. If you just remove the definition and the curly braces, as in Example 9.5, the program would work the same way, but read slightly differently.

Example 9.5: Code without the Procedure

```
(some text) 100 200 moveto show
```

This is a little unusual, because the data and instructions are not interleaved in a comfortable and readable fashion, as in Example 9.6.

Example 9.6: Data in a More Familiar Arrangement

```
100 200 moveto (some text) show
```

In a procedure body, you don't have the luxury of interleaving data and instructions, so you need to rearrange slightly the way data are presented to the procedure. You must pile all of the data up on the operand stack and use it piece by piece from within the procedure. Or you can simulate local

---

variables, and interleave the data and instructions in a familiar and readable way (see Example 9.7).

Example 9.7: Data Arrangement for Use by a Procedure

```
/S                          % Xloc Yloc (string) S -
{ %def
        /text exch def% string is on top of stack
        /Y exch def% Y and X reversed on stack
        /X exch def

        X Y moveto
        text show
} def
100 200 (some text) S
```

To some extent, the program has gotten more complicated in favor of readability. The last bit of the program, **X Y moveto text show**, is more readable than it was before, in the sense that the data and instructions are interleaved sensibly. However, this is at the expense of three pairs of **exch def** instructions and three name lookups for **X**, **Y**, and **text**.

There is a trade-off, in readability and efficiency, between creating these local names versus using data directly from the operand stack. If the data from the stack are used several times within the procedure, or if they are used in a very unusual order, significantly increased readability and a more easily maintained program can be constructed using the **exch def** approach. Otherwise the reduction in the number of operators executed and the number of name lookups required results in significantly improved performance.

TIP

A good rule of thumb is that if the operators within a procedure use each parameter just once or twice, it is better not to use local names for the parameters. Conversely, in a complicated procedure, it is usually better to choose sensible names for the parameters to heighten readability and to make the program more robust.

CONSTRUCTING GOOD PROCEDURES

Simplicity, readability, efficiency, and correctness are the most important aspects of your PostScript procedure, although not necessarily in that order. The overall size of a procedure body should be maintained as small as possible, but it is not more efficient to break a big procedure up into smaller ones to call by name from within the larger one, due to the additional name lookup and overhead on the execution stack.

What to Name Your Procedure

Assuming that you will create a procedure to be used by the rest of your program, you will typically give it a name and invoke it by that name. Of course, as with any programming language, the name should reflect the functionality of the procedure as much as possible. Select poor names for your smaller procedures and you may in fact make the program much less readable.

In choosing a name, it is important to consider just how the procedure will be used. If the procedure will be used in the "script" of a document and be invoked hundreds of times, its name should be short, to save space and time in the execution of the program. However, if the procedure is called only from other procedures that you have defined, you gain very little by giving it a short name, since the name is represented by a *name object* of fixed size once the procedure body has been constructed.

Let's consider some examples. Can you guess what the procedure called **p** does in Example 9.8?

Example 9.8: Disorganized and Inefficient Use of Procedures

```
/b { bind def } bind def      /d { def } b
/x { exch } b
/m { moveto } b
/r { rlineto } b
/c { closepath } b
/f { fill } b
/p { %def
       /#4 x d /#3 x d /#2 x d /#1 x d
       #3 #4 m #1 0 r 0 #2 r #1 neg 0 r c f
} b
100 100 400 50 p
```

It is difficult to decipher all the short names for operators given in Example 9.8, and the function of the program segment becomes less clear as a result. Furthermore, the program is very inefficient, since each of the short names actually invokes a procedure call (and therefore requires a fair amount of overhead).

The procedure in Example 9.9 does the same thing as the one in Example 9.8 but it takes much less time, is more readable, and occupies less memory.

Example 9.9: Efficient Procedure

```
/rectfill                    % Xloc Yloc Width Height rectfill
{ %def
        /Height exch def
        /Width exch def
        /Yloc exch def
        /Xloc exch def
        Xloc Yloc moveto
        Width 0 rlineto
        0 Height rlineto
        Width neg 0 rlineto
        closepath fill
} bind def
400 50 100 100 rectfill
```

Also, for comparison, Example 9.10 presents the same program without any local names defined for the arguments:

Example 9.10: Efficient Procedure without Local Names

```
/rectfill                    % Xloc Yloc Width Height rectfill
{ %def
        4 -2 roll moveto
        1 index 0 rlineto
        0 exch rlineto
        neg 0 rlineto
        closepath fill
} bind def
400 50 100 100 rectfill
```

The purpose of this procedure is much more clear now, since the native PostScript operators can be seen easily, and since the names chosen for the procedure and its arguments are intuitive and make sense. The original example, even though it used local names for all of the arguments, was extremely difficult to understand, mostly because the names were poorly chosen. The last example, without any local names at all, is much easier to follow thanks to the native PostScript operator names. Example 9.9 is probably the easiest of all to understand. Interestingly enough, the only way it differs from Example 9.8 is in the names chosen (and in the indentation style).

Some of the very most difficult programs to understand are those that define hundreds of two-letter names for procedures and have each procedure call three others, making it almost impossible to trace the execution of the program, to cut pieces from it, to maintain it, or to understand it.

A Useful Naming Convention

To cement the ideas behind good naming of procedures and variables, following is an example of a naming convention that can help keep it all straight. You may adopt your own naming conventions, of course.

- Use lower-case letters only for procedure names, since they behave more or less like the PostScript built-in operators, which are all lower-case.
- Use mixed-case for variables, like **/LeftMargin** or **/FontSize**.
- If the procedure names are never transmitted in quantity (as they might be in the body of a document), there is no reason to make them short. The interpreter will make them into tokens anyway.
- Use single-letter names for the most commonly called procedures in the body (or script) of a document, keeping them as mnemonic as possible. For example, use **/s** for show, **/f** for setting the font, **/c** for curves, and so on.
- For procedures that are called frequently in the script of a document but which are not the "workhorses," use two-letter names rather than using one-letter names that are not mnemonic. For example, it is better to use **/ml** for **{ moveto lineto }** than to use, say, **/q**.
- For procedures that are called from within other procedures, use descriptive names like **/newline** or **/reencodefont**.

- Be very careful not to inadvertently redefine any built-in operators. Common names that are accidentally used by programmers include **begin**, **end**, **print**, and **lt** (which seems natural for **lineto**, but which is already used for less-than).

SELF-MODIFYING PROCEDURES

This is a pretty fancy concept, "self-modifying procedures." It invites thoughts either of artificial intelligence or of assembly language techniques that are usually discouraged. However, in a simpler form, self-modifying procedures can be extremely useful—without being dangerously difficult.

Since a PostScript procedure is just an array, it is relatively easy to change the contents. It is just a matter of using array operations. Let's look at a practical example. When using the **settransfer** operator to set up a gray-level transfer function, it is correct to add your function to the end of the transfer function that is already in place, rather than to replace it. Let's assume that the existing transfer function exchanges black for white, as in Example 9.11.

Example 9.11: Existing Transfer Function

{1 exch sub }

This is a simple function that inverts the sense of black and white. Let's imagine that you want to set another transfer function that makes a single exception of black and makes it 50 percent gray instead (see Example 9.12).

Example 9.12: New Transfer Function to be Set

{ dup 0 eq { pop 0.5 } if }

To concatenate the two procedures, you would want a result in which both procedures are executed in order (see Example 9.13).

Example 9.13: Resulting Transfer Function

```
{ 1 exch sub dup 0 eq { pop 0.5 } if }
```

But in order to do this, you must know the size of the existing transfer function, allocate a new array, and copy the contents of both the old and the new functions into the third array. This is both time-consuming and uses storage space inefficiently.

Let's look at an alternative that is predicated on modifying a procedure body as if it were just an array. Strictly speaking, this is not a self-modifying procedure, but shares the notion of creating new procedure bodies from existing ones (Example 9.14).

Example 9.14: Invoking the Old Function from the New One

```
{ OLD exec dup 0 eq { pop 0.5 } if }
dup currenttransfer exch 0 exch put
settransfer
```

This is a bit tricky, but it has a simple underlying concept. You want the new procedure simply to execute the old one before it starts, which could be done with the **exec** operator if you had the object to **exec**. The trick is that the new transfer function is created with a dummy element as the argument to **exec**. The name **OLD** is not a name that is defined anywhere, but since the procedure has not yet been executed, it is okay to put any name into it. The trick is to replace that name with the actual body of the existing transfer function. The **exec** that immediately follows will then execute it. The advantage to this approach is that you don't have to allocate a new array, and since all procedures are represented by a single PostScript object, you can always replace the name **OLD** with the object that represents the entire previous transfer function.

In Example 9.14, the **currenttransfer** operator produces the existing procedure object on the operand stack. The fancy **dup currenttransfer exch 0 exch put** code just inserts that procedure object into location **0** of the new procedure array, and carefully leaves a copy of the procedure body on the stack when done. (That's what the instances of **dup** accomplish.) The net result, in memory in the interpreter, looks something like Figure 9.1.

Figure 9.1: Object Pointer in a Procedure Body

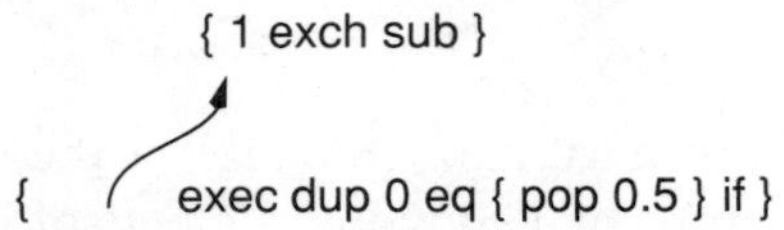

```
        { 1 exch sub }

        ↗
{       / exec dup 0 eq { pop 0.5 } if }
```

An interesting example of self-modifying code is a procedure that does something only once, the first time it is called, then redefines itself so that the action will not be repeated. Example 9.15 uses this technique to set up the font and point size the first time the text-setting procedure is called, but it redefines itself not to bother setting up the font each time thereafter.

Example 9.15: Procedure that Redefines Itself

```
/S                            % (string) Xloc Yloc S -
{ %def
        % initialization code, only done once:
        /Times-Roman 12 selectfont
        0 setgray
        % now carry out the task and redefine self:
        moveto show
        /S { moveto show } def
} bind def
(some text) 100 600 S
(more text) 100 587 S
```

This is not necessarily recommended practice, but demonstrates a fairly useful technique that can be used when other methods of initialization are not possible. For example, you could change the behavior of an existing document by redefining a procedure that was called by the document, even if you could not add additional procedure calls to the document itself.

CONCLUDING THOUGHTS

Procedures are executable arrays. This gives you the power to execute array operations on them occasionally, to copy them, to add elements, or to replace dummy objects with real ones. Procedure bodies are also used as arguments to many PostScript operators. Since the procedure bodies used by the **ifelse** operator are no different than ones you might define for your own use, you can use the same techniques, apply **bind** to them, or dynamically replace them with something else.

The PostScript procedure mechanism is extremely powerful and flexible, and with your new and increasing understanding of the way procedures work, you should be able to put them to good use in your own programs. The next chapter opens still more possibilities, as it explains the use of dictionaries for various purposes in PostScript.

EXERCISES

1. Replace the following PostScript sequence with an equivalent one that makes use of a single procedure call named **TEXT** instead of the in-line PostScript operators.

```
100 100 moveto
/Times-Bold findfont 24 scalefont setfont
(This is an example of Times-Bold) show
```

2. Write a procedure that takes two procedure bodies and concatenates them into a third procedure body, which it leaves on the stack. Call your procedure **concatprocs**.

3. Rewrite the **def** operator as a procedure that has the same functionality, but don't use **def** within your procedure. (HINT: You must use another PostScript operator to accomplish the same thing.) It's okay to use **def** to define your procedure, but it should not contain the **def** operator.

4. Redefine the **moveto** operator to check for operands that are off the page, and to report these errant coordinates with the == operator. Use a page size of 612 by 792 points, and don't worry about a scaled coordinate system.

Chapter 10

Using Dictionaries

Dictionaries are the basic form of storage in the PostScript language. Whenever you use the **def** operator, you are storing something into a dictionary. Each time you use a name like **moveto** or call up one of your procedures named **L**, you are retrieving data out of a dictionary.

To fully understand how dictionaries store data, it is necessary to realize that all PostScript data types are represented by objects. These objects are all the same size, even if the data that they represent are too big to fit inside the object. A dictionary is a place to make key–value pairs of objects. (Remember: the value is the object you want to store, and the key is the name under which you store it.) To get the value back, you need the key again. If your value is a composite object (such as a string, an array, or another dictionary) the data will actually be in memory that has been previously allocated to hold it, and the object stored in the dictionary points to it. Example 10.1 is a simple example of a dictionary entry.

Example 10.1: Sample Dictionary Entry

```
/redraw                        % strokegray fillgray redraw -
{ %def
      gsave
            setgray myuserpath ufill
            setgray myuserpath ustroke
      grestore
} def
```

In this case, the object that is stored as the value is the procedure body **{ gsave setgray myuserpath ufill setgray myuserpath ustroke grestore }**, and the key under which it is stored is the name **redraw**.

TIP

The memory used for storage of PostScript objects is allocated when the object is created, not when it is stored into a dictionary. The dictionary must have room for the definition in it already; only the two objects representing the key and the value are actually saved in the dictionary. In Example 10.1, the procedure body consumes about 72 bytes of memory when it is created, but no additional memory is used when it is stored into the dictionary with **def**.

DICTIONARIES FOR NAME SCOPING

Name scoping involves making names context-sensitive, depending on the dictionaries currently on the dictionary stack. To understand its usefulness, you must know that the most common method for retrieving data that have been stored into a dictionary is to use the *name lookup* mechanism. With this mechanism, an executable name encountered by the interpreter is looked up in the context of the current dictionary stack. You can use a key more than once and it can have different values associated with it in different dictionaries. When the name is looked up, the dictionary stack is searched from the top down, and the first instance of the key that is encountered is the one that is used.

This provides a simple mechanism for changing name scoping. As an example, consider the problem of underlining text. You may want to have a simple text-setting procedure that you use when you're not underlining (which is most of the time, usually), and a different procedure that you use when you are underlining. One way to approach that might be to have a separate dictionary with underlining information that gets pushed onto the dictionary stack when you want to underline (Example 10.2).

Example 10.2: Using Dictionary to Control Name Scoping

```
% these procedure turn underlining on and off by
% pushing the underlinedict dictionary on the dict stack
% or popping it off:
/underlineON { underlinedict begin } def
/underlineOFF { end } def

% here is a sample regular definition for "S":
/regulardict 4 dict def
regulardict begin   % (string) /Font size Xloc Yloc S
        /S { moveto selectfont show } bind def
end

% alternate definition for "S" that does underlining:
/underlinedict 4 dict def
underlinedict begin
        /S                      % (string) Xloc Yloc S –
        { %def
                moveto selectfont currentpoint 3 -1 roll show
                0 UnderLinePosition neg rmoveto
                UnderLinePosition sub lineto stroke
        } bind def     % (or whatever)
end
```

LOCAL DICTIONARIES

A *local dictionary* is a dictionary that is visible only under certain circumstances. If a procedure body references a particular dictionary, it is said to be local to that procedure body.

Local dictionaries are very useful. One of the most common uses of a local dictionary is to store local definitions that might be used by a procedure. This is especially important if you use the **def** operator, which writes into the current dictionary. It is best to make sure you know where all of the definitions are being made, to prevent errors like **dictfull** or **invalidaccess**.

Example 10.3 shows the most common technique for using local dictionaries for temporary storage for procedures. There are two things worthy of note in this example.

1. The dictionary is created (allocated) outside of the procedure itself. This keeps it from being created each time the procedure is called.

2. The same dictionary is shared among several procedures, since the data storage is only temporary. Even though the names **X** and **Y** are defined by both procedures, they do not interfere with one another as long as the use of those names does not go outside the scope of the procedure.

Example 10.3: Dictionary as Local Storage for a Procedure

```
/LOCAL 5 dict def    % one dictionary used by all procedures

/Text                       % (string) Xloc Yloc Text -
{ %def
      LOCAL begin
             /X exch def
             /Y exch def
             /text exch def
             X Y moveto text show
      end
} bind def
/Box                        % X Y Width Height Box -
{ %def
      LOCAL begin
             /Height exch def
             /Width exch def
             /Y exch def
             /X exch def
             X Y moveto
             Width 0 rlineto
             0 Height rlineto
             Width neg 0 rlineto
             closepath stroke
      end
} bind def
```

In Example 10.3, the **LOCAL** dictionary stores only the data, and the procedures themselves are simply written into the current dictionary.

GLOBAL DICTIONARIES OF PROCEDURES

The only time you really need local dictionaries is for re-entrant code or recursion. For most other situations, a good approach is to create one larger dictionary to hold both procedures and their data, as long as you are careful about name conflicts (Example 10.3). They are not really "local variables," but if you need to be careful about storage space but are not worried about recursion or name conflict within your own code, this is much simpler and more efficient. This technique also relieves each procedure of having to **begin** and **end** the dictionary, which makes it easier to maintain and faster at the same time.

TIP

Most PostScript drivers and any program with more than a small handful of procedures should make sure to build its own dictionary for storing the procedures, to avoid the **dictfull** error that might result if you trust the execution environment to have enough room in, say, the **userdict** dictionary for all your definitions.

Example 10.3 shows the use of a single dictionary for all definitions made by the program. This technique can be a little bit riskier, since there is still a chance that another dictionary might be left on top of **ProductDict** (perhaps by an included illustration); this would make all subsequent instances of **def** write into the wrong dictionary. However, you can make sure to check the dictionary stack whenever you include an illustration. This technique is the best general approach for storing definitions in a private dictionary.

Example 10.4: All Procedures within One Global Dictionary

```
/ProductDict 7 dict def

ProductDict begin
        /Text                   % (string) Xloc Yloc Text -
        { %def
                /X exch def
                /Y exch def
                /text exch def
                X Y moveto text show
        } bind def
```

```
        /Box                % X Y Width Height Box -
        { %def
                /Height exch def
                /Width exch def
                /Y exch def
                /X exch def
                X Y moveto
                Width 0 rlineto
                0 Height rlineto
                Width neg 0 rlineto
                closepath stroke
} bind def
end %ProductDict

%%BeginSetup
        % make sure "ProductDict" is available at run time:
        ProductDict begin
%%EndSetup
%%Trailer
        % make sure to remove "ProductDict" when done:
        end  %ProductDict
%%EOF
```

MAINTAINING THE DICTIONARY STACK

The dictionary stack in a PostScript interpreter is not as readily manipulated as the operand stack. There are no equivalent operators for the dictionary stack operators such as **exch**, **roll**, and **dup**. The only way to rearrange dictionaries is to place them temporarily on the operand stack, rearrange them there, then replace them on the dictionary stack.

For the most part, it should not be necessary to rearrange the dictionaries on the dictionary stack, but it is occasionally important to make sure your dictionary is the topmost one. In these circumstances, it might be best to simply use **begin** to explicitly place your dictionary on the top, even if it might already be present further down on the dictionary stack.

Example 10.5 presents a procedure to implement **dictexch**, the equivalent of the **exch** operator for the dictionary stack. This example is intended to give you the flavor of the necessary dictionary manipulation; to see how it works, see Example 10.5. The procedure shown is not necessarily a recommended approach for using the dictionary stack.

Example 10.5 Exchanging Topmost Dictionaries with *dictexch*

```
/dictexch              % - dictexch -
{ %def
      currentdict end    % dictionary A moved to operand stack
      currentdict end    % dictionary B moved
      exch               % exchange A and B on operand stack
      begin              % dictionary A back on dictionary stack
      begin              % dictionary B is now on top
} bind def
```

Figure 10.1: Mechanics of the *dictexch* Procedure

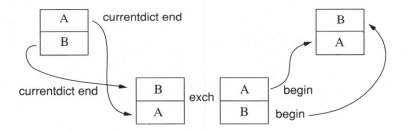

One of the most important aspects of maintaining the dictionary stack is to make sure you remove any dictionaries that you may have put onto the dictionary stack. The mechanism for doing this is the **end** operator, which pops the topmost dictionary off the dictionary stack. Make sure you have thought through any potential conflicts with other programs, embedded illustrations, or other code that might add or subtract dictionaries from the dictionary stack. It is usually best to remove your local dictionaries from the stack before transferring control to an embedded program, then reinstating them when you get control back.

The PostScript dictionary stack operations are not as powerful or flexible as those for the operand stack. The dictionary stack is intended for lighter-duty manipulation, and to provide a strong mechanism for name lookup and storage. Keep this in the back of your mind if you are thinking of writing a **dictroll**, **dictdup**, or other procedure just for this purpose.

INTO AND OUT OF DICTIONARIES

The dictionary stack holds dictionary objects. There are built-in operators in the PostScript language for putting things into or retrieving things from the current dictionary. There are also several other ways to manipulate the contents of dictionaries directly.

A dictionary is a normal PostScript object and can exist on the operand stack as well as on the dictionary stack. The **put** operator lets you put an entry directly into a dictionary that is on the operand stack, and **get** lets you retrieve from it. (See Example 10.6.)

Example 10.6: Using *put* and *get* for Dictionary Entries

```
/MyFont        % leave on operand stack
15 dict        % leave on operand stack
      dup /FontName /MyFont put
      dup /Encoding StandardEncoding put
      dup /BuildChar { whatever } put
      dup /CharStrings 100 dict put
definefont pop


% This is not the recommended way to call an operator:
statusdict /ledgertray get exec
systemdict /showpage get exec
```

If your needs are simple, you may be able to avoid having to place a local dictionary on the operand stack at all. You can use the **get** and **put** operators to explicitly reference a dictionary without ever placing it on the dictionary stack. In Example 10.7, the save object that results from executing **save** is stored away into a dictionary, and is retrieved later for restore. Since there is only a single entry to be written into the dictionary, it is a little bit simpler (although perhaps no clearer) to use **put** rather than **begin**, **def**, and **end**.

Example 10.7: Scoping with *put* and *get*

```
userdict /mysaveobj save put
   % embedded illustration here
userdict /mysaveobj get restore
```

LOOKING INTO DICTIONARIES

Dictionaries contain key–value pairs. In addition to being able to retrieve specific entries from a dictionary with the **get** or **load** operator, you can see what entries already exist in the dictionary with the **forall** operator. This can be useful for various purposes, such as finding out what fonts are currently defined in the interpreter (looking in the **FontDirectory** or **SharedFontDirectory** dictionaries) or in debugging, to figure out which dictionary is currently on top of the dictionary stack.

Using the **forall** Operator

Looking through existing dictionaries can be instructive, even if it isn't part of any production code you are writing. One of the most useful operators for this purpose is the **forall** operator. This operator loops through the contents of a dictionary and executes your procedure for each key–value pair found in the dictionary. Example 10.8 shows a simple way to enumerate a dictionary with the **forall** operator.

Example 10.8: Browsing a Dictionary with *forall*

```
/browse-dict                 % dictionary browse-dict –
{ %def
       { %forall
              exch   % name first
              (key: ) print ==
              (val: ) print ==
       } forall
} bind def
userdict browse-dict
```

The entries will not come out in a particularly sensible order. Instead, they are in *hash table* order, in which the location in the dictionary is determined by deriving an index directly from the key you used. (To digress slightly, an example hash function might be to add up the byte values of all the characters in a name object and use that number as an index into an array.) To make the **forall** operator a little more useful, you can use the **type** operator to take a look at each value in the dictionary, and take different measures depending on the data type. This will help to look into other dictionaries and arrays that might be lurking inside the dictionary you are perusing. But be careful if you use a recursive approach, since a dictionary may contain a reference to itself.

Example 10.9 shows another implementation of the **browse-dict** procedure; this implementation also browses subdictionaries and arrays. It uses the **type** operator to recognize these composite data types. This is much more complicated-looking code, mostly because of the inelegance of the **ifelse** constructs in the middle that are needed to check on the types of the data.

Example 10.9: Using *type* on each Element in a Dictionary

```
/browse-dict                  % dictionary browse-dict -
{ %def
      { %forall
            exch (key: ) print ==
            dup type
            dup /dicttype eq { %ifelse
                  (subdictionary: ) print
                  browse-dict              % recursively browse dictionary
            }{
                  (value: ) print ==
            } ifelse
      } forall
} bind def


/browse-array                 % array browse-array -
{ %def
      { %forall
            dup type
            dup /dicttype eq { %ifelse
                  (subdictionary: ) print
                  browse-dict   % recursively browse dictionary
            }{
                  dup /arraytype eq { %ifelse
                  (array: ) print
                  browse-array
                  }{ %else
                  (value: ) print ==
                  } ifelse
            } ifelse
      } forall
} bind def
```

Using the **where** and **known** Operators

A very good way to make sure your code is portable if you are using features that may or may not be present on all implementations is to use either the **known** or the **where** operators. These operators allow you to check for the existence of names in dictionaries, and execute some conditional code based on whether or not you find them.

For example, let's say you want to use four-color operations in the CMYK color space (cyan, magenta, yellow, and black). As a point of interest, the reason K is used by convention—rather than B—to represent black is that B is already used to represent the color blue in the RGB color model (red, green, blue).

You want to use the **setcmykcolor** operator, but if it isn't available, you can simulate it using **setrgbcolor**. Using the **where** operator, you can define a simulation only if the name **setcmykcolor** is not defined already in the interpreter (see Example 10.10).

Example 10.10: Conditionally Defining a Procedure

```
% /C points to "setcmykcolor" if it exists, else it emulates it with "setrgbcolor"
/C
      /setcmykcolor where { %ifelse
            /setcmykcolor get
      }{ %ifelse
            { %def
                  1 sub 3 { %repeat
                        3 index add neg dup 0 lt { pop 0 } if 3 1 roll
                  } repeat
                  setrgbcolor
            } bind
      } ifelse
def
```

In this case the **/C** is left on the operand stack while **where** is executed to determine whether or not the simulation is needed for **setcmykcolor**. If the name **setcmykcolor** is found, the current definition of it is loaded onto the operand stack. In either case, the name **/C** will have equivalent functionality to the **setcmykcolor** operator, and can be used throughout the program with the same arguments that **setcmykcolor** requires, without having to adjust the rest of the program according to the color model or the interpreter used.

REDEFINING OPERATORS

There are very often instances in which you want to change the behavior of your program, even just temporarily, by redefining some of the names in it before the program executes. This has many possible uses, for debugging, page accounting, distilling documents into another form, or adding to the functionality of an existing program.

As you have learned, name lookup is done in the context of the dictionary stack. There are correspondingly two basic ways to redefine a name non-destructively.

- Make a simple redefinition in the current dictionary with **def**.
- Push a special dictionary onto the dictionary stack into which the redefinitions are placed.

If you put the redefinitions in a separate dictionary, then it is easy to put them in place or remove them temporarily, simply by pushing or popping the dictionary from the dictionary stack. However, this method is a little bit more subject to problems, since the program may inadvertently remove your special dictionary from the dictionary stack, or try to write into it as if it were its own dictionary.

Changing the Behavior of Operators

When you redefine an operator to have some other behavior beyond or instead of its default, you must take care to preserve at least the way in which the operator interacts with the operand stack, and you probably need to simulate some of the side effects, as well. For example, the **moveto** operator pops two numbers off the stack and installs a current point into the graphics state. If you redefine **moveto**, you should at least make sure to pop exactly two numbers from the stack, and you probably ought to establish a current point while you're at it, if you want the program to continue to execute beyond the next instruction or so (without generating a **nocurrentpoint** error). One very good way to accomplish this is simply to invoke the original definition of the name when you are finished with your extensions. Example 10.11 shows a redefinition of **showpage** that adds a "draft" notice onto the edge of the document as it is being printed. The original (or previous, to be more accurate) definition of

showpage is loaded at the beginning, and is executed from within the redefined **showpage** procedure:

Example 10.11: Redefining *showpage* to Print Draft Notice

```
/startingCTM matrix currentmatrix def
/old_showpage /showpage load def
/showpage                  % - showpage -
{ %def
      gsave
              startingCTM setmatrix
              90 rotate 30 -590 moveto
              /Helvetica-Bold findfont 24 scalefont setfont
              (DRAFT document. Please destroy promptly.) show
      grestore
      old_showpage
} bind def
```

Debugging with Redefined Names

A very good way to track the execution of your program is to redefine one of the operations in it to produce some extra tracking information as it is being called. For instance, you could redefine the **show** operator to echo each string back to the standard output file as it is being printed, or you could redefine the **moveto** operator to watch for coordinates that are off the page and to warn you. Then, once you get the program working, you can simply remove your redefinitions, and the program should work without further modification.

Example 10.12 contains a simple redefinition of the **show** operator that will track each string as it is being printed.

Example 10.12: Redefining *show* to Help Debugging

```
/old_show /show load def
/show                      % (string) show -
{ %def
      dup == flush
      old_show
} bind def
```

Proper Nesting of Redefinitions

It is important to redefine names carefully so that they can be nested reasonably. It is always good to use the **load** operator when you pick up the old definition of a name. This is much better than, say, looking up the name directly in **systemdict**. However, it is also useful to keep your own name (like **/old_show**) from clobbering itself if you install your procedures a second time. One good way to accomplish that is to push a special dictionary onto the dictionary stack, but to avoid giving it a name (or your name will conflict with itself the second time you install the procedure). Example 10.13 illustrates this technique by loading the existing value stored under the name **show**, storing it away under the name **old_show**.

Example 10.13: Using *load* to Get Previous Definitions

```
/old_show /show load def
/show { %def
        dup == flush
        old_show
} bind def
```

CONCLUDING THOUGHTS

Dictionaries are flexible and powerful. The main uses for them are as storage for items that you don't want to leave on the operand stack and as a name lookup mechanism for scoping program execution or local variables. You have learned several ways to manipulate dictionaries, store and retrieve entries from dictionaries, and look at their contents. Dictionaries are not heavily used in most PostScript programs other than to store simple definitions, but they can be exploited for some interesting purposes when the need arises, as you have seen. In the next chapter, dictionaries are contrasted to arrays and various methods of creating and manipulating data are presented.

EXERCISES

1. What value is left on the operand stack after executing the following short program segment?

```
/variable 7 def
5 dict dup begin
    /variable 9 def
end
/variable dup load 3 1 roll get add
```

2. Replace the dictionary named **LOCALDICT** in the following procedure with an anonymous dictionary. (The dictionary itself should have no name, and the only instance of the dictionary object should be inside the procedure body.)

```
/LOCALDICT 12 dict def
/boxproc                % Xloc Yloc Width Height boxproc -
{ %def
    LOCALDICT begin
        /height exch def
        /width exch def
        /Y exch def
        /X exch def
        X Y moveto
        0 height rlineto
        width 0 rlineto
        0 height neg rlineto
        closepath
        fill
    end
} bind def
```

3. Name three operators in the PostScript language that use the dictionary stack in some way.

4. Write a program that shows (with the == operator) the names of all the fonts stored in the dictionary called **FontDirectory**.

Chapter 11

Creating and Manipulating Data

The two most basic types of data structures are arrays and strings. PostScript arrays can contain any other type of PostScript objects, including composite objects. Strings contain individual characters, as in most languages.

CONSTRUCTING AN ARRAY

To construct an array, the simplest thing to do is to use the [and] operators. These operators create an array on the fly, during the execution of your program, and put into that array anything that is on the operand stack down through the matching [at the time the] operator is executed. A simple example is seen in Example 11.1.

Example 11.1: Sample Constructed Array

[/one dup dup (four) /five 3 3 add /seven { 8 (the whole procedure) } 9 10]

This array contains ten elements:

```
/one        /one
/one        (four)
/five       6
/seven      { 8 (the whole procedure) }
 9          10
```

Notice that the second and third instances of /**one** were created by the execution of **dup** and the **6** was constructed by the **add** operator before the] was executed. The elements between the [and] operators are all executed, unlike the way procedure bodies are declared.

If you want to construct a literal array (the kind with [ ] brackets) that contains an executable name like **dup** or **add**, obviously you have to be careful, or the operators will actually execute instead of landing in your array. We could have created the array first as a procedure, taking advantage of the fact that the execution of objects inside the procedure is deferred, and then converted it to a literal array after it has been constructed (see Example 11.2).

Example 11.2: Making a Procedure into a Literal Array

{ /one dup dup 3 3 add } cvlit

The array generated from the executable procedure body is identical to one that might be constructed with the [and] operators. It contains six elements:

```
/one        dup
dup         3
3           add
```

Another way to construct an array is to create an empty one with the **array** operator, and put data into it yourself with the **put** or **putinterval** operators, or with the **astore** operator, as seen in Example 11.3.

Example 11.3: Creating and Filling an Empty Array

```
10 array dup
/one /one /one (four) /five
6 /seven { 8 (the whole procedure) } 9 10
astore
```

CONSTRUCTING A STRING

Strings can be constructed in much the same way as arrays. You can create one at run-time in the original input program by using the notation found in Example 11.4 for simple strings or hexadecimal strings (also called hex strings).

Example 11.4: Creating Strings with the Scanner

```
(This is a string created at run-time; following is a hex string:)
<a32989e4ff>
```

Hexadecimal strings are scanned two bytes at a time to create the single byte represented by the 8-bit number. (One byte of hexadecimal, since it is base 16, provides only 4 bits of data; it requires two bytes of hexadecimal to represent a full 8 bits.) Hex strings are generally used only for image data, strings for Kanji character sets, or other places where full 8-bit string data must be used. The **string** operator can also be used to create an empty string body, and you can use **put** or **putinterval** to put bytes into the string.

MANIPULATING DATA WITH **PUT** AND **GET**

Strings and arrays are composite data structures. They are both represented by single objects, but really they are composed of collections of objects. There are a few different ways to read and write the contents of these composite data structures, included in Table 11.1. The fundamental mechanism is the family of **put** and **get** operators. We'll start with the simplest ones.

Table 11.1: Operators to *put* and *get* Data

Arguments	Operator	Action
array	**length** *int*	number of elements in *array*
array index	**get** *any*	get *array* element indexed by *index*
array index any	**put**	put *any* into *array* at *index*
array index count	**getinterval** *subarray*	subarray of *array* starting at *index* for *count* elements
$array_1$ *index* $array_2$	**putinterval**	replace subarray of $array_1$ starting at index by $array_2$
array	**aload** $a_0...a_{n-1}$ *array*	push all elements of *array* on stack
$any_0 ... any_{n-1}$ *array*	**astore** *array*	pop elements from stack into array
$array_1$ $array_2$	**copy** $subarray_2$	copy elements of $array_1$ to initial subarray of *array2*
array proc	**forall**	execute proc for each element of array
int	**string** *string*	create *string* of length *int*
string	**length** *int*	returns the number of elements in *string*
string index	**get** *int*	get *string* element indexed by *index*
string index int	**put**	put *int* into *string* at *index*
string index count	**getinterval** *substring*	substring of *string* starting at *index* for *count* elements
$string_1$ *index* $string_2$	**putinterval**	replace substring of $string_1$ starting at *index* by $string_2$
$string_1$ $string_2$	**copy** $substring_2$	copy elements of $string_1$ to initial substring of $string_2$

The **put** operator requires three arguments: the thing you want data put into, the key or position in that composite data structure where you want the data put, and finally the piece of data itself that is to be added (see Example 11.5).

Example 11.5: Anatomy of the *put* Operator

```
% data_structure position_key new_data put
currentdict /key (value) put
10 array 0 (first element) put
(XXXXX) 4 (a) put
```

The **putinterval** operator is similar to **put**, but the piece of data you supply needs to be of the same type as the data structure into which you are putting it. The data gets copied from the supplied data into the destination, rather than putting just one piece of data (see Example 11.6).

Example 11.6: Anatomy of the *putinterval* Operator

```
data_structure position_key data_structure putinterval
12 array 5 [ /f /g /h /i /j /k ] putinterval
(abcDEF) 0 (ABC) putinterval
```

TIP If you have difficulty remembering the order of operands to the **put** and **get** operators, remember that they work in the same order that **def** and **load** take their operands: the key comes before the value.

CONCATENATING ARRAYS AND STRINGS

Arrays and strings have a fixed length. You cannot dynamically extend them. In order to tack two of them together, you must allocate a third array or string that is big enough to hold the other two, then copy them both into it. There is no easier way to do it, unfortunately.

Example 11.7 sets forth a procedure called **concatenate**. This **concatenate** procedure tacks together two string bodies into a third string that is left on the operand stack as the result of the procedure call. The procedure works with arrays in precisely the same way. If you copy this example, be careful not to call it **concat**, since that is the name of another PostScript operator for concatenating matrices.

The **roll** operator is used in the body of this procedure to avoid having to make any dictionary entries. This is intentional, since a procedure used as an operator-equivalent (as **concatenate** is) should have as few side effects as possible.

Note the use of **putinterval** in this procedure. It is called once to copy the body of the first argument into the destination at position 0, then it is called a second time with the position in the destination equal to the length of the first argument, so the second argument lands exactly where the first part left off. Note the use of **length** to determine this position, and the careful use of **dup** and **index** to keep copies of the various strings or arrays until we are done with them. The **length**, **putinterval**, and **type** operators all consume their operands, so you must take care to operate on a copy of the original arguments until they are no longer needed.

Example 11.7: Concatenating Two Strings Together

```
/concatenate              % (string1) (string2) concatenate string3
                          % array1 array2 concatenate array3
{ %def
       dup type 2 index type 2 copy ne { %if
              pop pop
              errordict begin (concatenate) typecheck end
       }{ %else
              /stringtype ne exch /arraytype ne and {
                     errordict begin (concatenate) typecheck end
              } if
       } ifelse
       dup length 2 index length add 1 index type
       /arraytype eq { array }{ string } ifelse
       % stack: arg1 arg2 new
       dup 0 4 index putinterval
       % stack: arg1 arg2 new
       dup 4 -1 roll length 4 -1 roll putinterval
       % stack: new
} bind def
(string1) (string2) concatenate ==
[ /zero /one /two ] [ /three /four /five /six ] concatenate ==
```

INPUT AND OUTPUT OF STRING DATA

A string is basically a chunk of memory in which characters are stored. The string body is created first, then characters may be added to it with the **copy**, **put**, **putinterval**, **read**, **readstring**, or **readhexstring** operators.

There are two primary sources for string data. The most commonly used one is to supply the data as a literal string (using the familiar parentheses), as shown in Example 11.8.

Example 11.8: Creating a Literal String

```
% normal "show" string:
(This is a string) show
% exactly the same result using a hex string:
<54686973206973206120737472696e67> show
```

The scanner allocates a string body of the appropriate size and copies the bytes into it for you, leaving a string object on the top of the operand stack. The string is delimited by parentheses, and can contain parentheses if they are quoted with a backslash character before the parens, like this:

(some \) parens in a \(string body).

The other main source of string data, other than synthetically created strings, is a file object. You can open a file and read bytes directly into string bodies, but the strings must have been allocated beforehand. Example 11.9 shows this quite well.

Example 11.9: Reading String Data from a File

```
/buffer 128 string def
currentfile buffer readline % reads directly from input
This is a string
show

% read through /etc/password and print line containing "Glenn"
/buffer 128 string def
/passwd (/etc/passwd) (r) file def
{ %loop
 passwd buffer readline {
        dup (Glenn) search {
                pop pop pop
                print(\n) print flush
                exit
        }{ pop } ifelse
 }{ exit } ifelse
} loop
passwd closefile
```

ARRAYS VERSUS DICTIONARIES

There are several differences between arrays and dictionaries that make them more (or less) appropriate for a given task. The most important differences are:

- Arrays can be accessed sequentially, but dictionaries cannot be accessed sequentially (the **forall** operator uses hash table order).

- Dictionary access can be made automatic using name lookup. By contrast, the only way to retrieve something from an array is with **get** or **getinterval**.

- Arrays need about half the memory that dictionaries require, since there is no key to be stored.

- Arrays can be created dynamically, without having to know ahead of time how many entries may be needed.

It is unfortunately very common for programs to allocate huge dictionaries but never to use all the space that was allocated. This is often a result of the debugging cycle, when a dictionary was made large in response to a **dictfull** error or in anticipation of larger program growth. This is easily enough avoided, of course, but it is common enough that it is worth mention.

As a rule of thumb, if the data you need to store are needed sequentially or all of the entries are needed at once, you are better off using arrays than dictionaries. Dictionaries are most powerful for storing procedures and variables for your program, and have only specialized applications for the data that is used by a program.

ADVANCED TECHNIQUES

PostScript programs that read data directly from a file sometimes have to perform extensive string manipulation to use the data. An interesting trick for parsing data is to use the **token** operator. If your data are ASCII and can be interpreted somehow as PostScript-like objects, your parsing task can be greatly simplified.

Consider the program in Example 11.10 that reads pairs of points from the input file and constructs line segments from them. The output of this example is shown in Figure 11.1.

Example 11.10: Reading and Executing Data from a File

```
%!PS-Adobe-2.0 EPSF-2.0
%%BoundingBox: 0 0 150 150
%%EndComments
100 300 translate
```

```
/buff 256 string def
{ %loop
        % assumes no errors in the data...
        currentfile buff readline not { exit } if
        (%%EOF) anchorsearch { exit } if
        token pop exch token pop exch 3 1 roll moveto
        token pop exch token pop exch pop lineto
        stroke
} bind loop
96 17 20 30
15.5 75.25 120 145.789
30 89.75 168.5 76.5
80 40 60 140
%%EOF
```

Figure 11.1: Output of Example 11.10

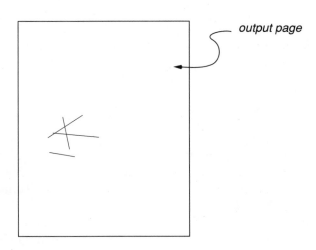

output page

CONCLUDING THOUGHTS

In this chapter, you've seen how to construct arrays and strings and how to manipulate them with **put** and **get**. You have also seen how to concatenate arrays and strings and how to do some simple and powerful manipulation of the data.

The PostScript language is not particularly strong in string-handling operations compared to some other languages, but it has all the necessary ingredients to do very respectable string manipulation when necessary.

When you work with arrays and strings, the most important thing to remember is that they are composite objects and work more like pointers than actual bodies of data. If you can keep track of when you need to copy the whole string or the whole array, you will have few problems with this kind of data manipulation.

In the next chapter you will see more in-depth treatment of the basics of data storage and retrieval and how to build data structures and use dictionaries creatively.

EXERCISES

1. What are the contents of the array constructed by the following code?

    ```
    [ 0 0 moveto 100 100 lineto currentpoint ]
    ```

2. Show the PostScript code to create a two-dimensional array five elements wide and ten elements deep.

3. The **filenameforall** operator is very useful in obtaining a list of font files written to the disk on a printer. However, the file names that the operator returns are of the form **(fonts/Palatino-Roman)** rather than simply **(Palatino-Roman)**. Write a procedure called **extractfontname** that will take a string like **(fonts/Palatino-Roman)** as input and strip off the **(fonts/)** part of the name, leaving just **(Palatino-Roman)**.

Chapter 12

Storing and Using Data

There are various kinds of data that get used by computer programs. Some programs "crunch" data, bent on achieving a particular result based on its input. Other programs allow users to create, edit, or rearrange data; the result is up to the user's imagination. Still others use input data only to guide them through labyrinthine paths, producing no results at all.

When writing your own program, it is worth considering just what the numbers and text will be used for before you decide on your data structures. For example, if your program takes a sequence of numbers and plots them, you probably don't want to store the numbers in a permanent place. In fact, the sooner you get rid of them (plot them), the better. However, many bits of data are in fact used internally by the program itself, to establish state, and are never intended as part of any output. (These bits of data may include, for example, the current page margins, the point size of the font you are using, or maybe a string buffer needed for reading from a file object.)

Data and the Operand Stack

Remember that all PostScript operators require their operands to be on the stack. Even if you store something into a dictionary, it must eventually get put back on the operand stack before it can be used for anything.

Of course, the operand stack is also the first place any data land on the way into your program. Assembling these ideas in our minds, we realize that maybe, under some circumstances, the data should just stay on the operand stack until they are used. That is the first principle of data storage and use in PostScript programming.

The exaggerated instance shown in Example 12.1 is a procedure that requires several operands, all of which are eventually used by some PostScript operators internally. In this example, these operands are given names within the procedure body, ostensibly so that the procedure will be easier to maintain. But notice that the values are no sooner stored into a dictionary than they are recalled onto the operand stack, which is unnecessarily slow.

Example 12.1: Using Too Many Variables

```
% This program draws a shaded, outlined box
/BX                    % X Y Bwidth Bheight fillgray linewidth linegray BX
{ %def
        /linegray exch def
        /linewidth exch def
        /boxgray exch def
        /Bheight exch def
        /Bwidth exch def
        /Y exch def
        /X exch def
        fillgray setgray
        X Y Bwidth Bheight rectfill
        linegray setgray
        linewidth setlinewidth
        X Y Bwidth Bheight rectstroke
} bind def
```

In this example, variables are created to hold data that are inherently transitory. The data really represent the box itself, and are not used by the program in any other way. To give them names and make them into variables has no purpose other than to make the program a bit more readable and easier to maintain. But the important lesson is to actually stop and consider how the data are being used, and design your data use to match that use.

Data and Algorithms for Underlining

Let's look at a slightly more involved example, one that is not quite so easy a choice. We need to underline some text on the page, and must keep track of the location and thickness that the underline should be. This is a typical situation that comes up when writing the PostScript printer driver for a word processor. We know where the underline for the text will start, since it is very closely related to the place where the text starts that you want to underline. It is a little more trouble to determine where the underlining should end, since you have to calculate exactly where the end of the text is, taking the font and point size into account as well as any kerning or other positioning decisions you may have made. Very likely, your word processor already has this information on hand, since it had to set the text. You also have to decide how far below the text the line should be, and how thick a line to use.

It is a simple matter to draw a horizontal line. In fact, all you need to know are its end points and how thick it should be. But the data that represent that line are actually derived from something else, namely the text being underlined.

A common model for underlining in a word processor is to have what amounts to "underline ON" and "underline OFF" commands, and have the program automatically underline whatever you type while the underlining is turned on. Let's suppose our PostScript driver models that behavior exactly (see Example 12.2).

Example 12.2: Simple Model for Underlining Text

```
/underlineON { /underline true def } def
/underlineOFF { /underline false def } def
```

These procedures simply set an internal variable in the program, called **underline**, to either **true** or **false**. But this variable must be noticed by the text-setting routines. First, let's look at the way we would like to use these procedures. We'll assume that a simple text-setting procedure definition is in place (see Example 12.3).

Example 12.3: Sample Use of this Underlining Model

```
% not yet fully functional, but illustrates the desired syntax
/underlineON { /underline true def } def
/underlineOFF { /underline false def } def
/TEXT { moveto show } def

/Times-Bold 24 selectfont
underlineON
(Hamlet, Act II) 200 650 TEXT
underlineOFF

/Times-Roman 12 selectfont
(This should be the first line from Hamlet.) 72 600 TEXT
(And this, of course, the second.) 72 570 TEXT
```

This example, unfortunately, won't draw any underlines yet, but it shows the use of the **underlineON** and **underlineOFF** procedures.

In our example driver, we don't want to have to change our use of the **TEXT** procedure to use underlining, we just want to be able to turn underlining on or off whenever the command is issued from the word processor. Of course, somewhere along the way the underlining has to actually happen. In this case, the **TEXT** procedure must check the underline flag to see if it is supposed to underline the text, and it must also calculate the appropriate parameters and location for the text itself (Example 12.4).

Example 12.4: Fleshing Out the Underlining Code

```
/underlineON { /underline true def } def
/underlineOFF { /underline false def } def
/TEXT { %def
      underline { %ifelse
      }{ %else
            moveto show
      } ifelse
} bind def
```

So far, this doesn't seem too bad, since only a single test has been added to our **TEXT** procedure. Of course, it still doesn't do any underlining, because the other half of the **ifelse** statement is still empty. Let's expand

---

the **underline** clause, just to see what kinds of variables or data are produced in calculating the underlining parameters (see Example 12.5).

Example 12.5: Actually Drawing the Underlines

```
/underlineON { /underline true def } def
/underlineOFF { /underline false def } def
/SCALE { 1000 div 24 mul } bind def
/TEXT                  % (string) Xloc Yloc TEXT -
{ %def
      underline { %ifelse
            moveto
            gsave
                  currentfont /FontInfo known { %ifelse
                        currentfont /FontInfo get begin
                              0 UnderlinePosition SCALE rmoveto
                              UnderlineThickness SCALE setlinewidth
                        end
                  }{ %else
                        0 -10 rmoveto 0.5 setlinewidth
                  } ifelse
                  dup stringwidth rlineto stroke
            grestore
            show
      }{ %else
            moveto show
      } ifelse
} bind def

/Times-Bold 24 selectfont
underlineON
(Hamlet, Act II) 200 650 TEXT
underlineOFF

/Times-Roman 12 selectfont
(This should be the first line from Hamlet.) 72 600 TEXT
(And this, of course, the second.) 72 570 TEXT
```

This is quite a bit more involved than the version without underlining, but most of it is fluff (**ifelse** statements, curly braces, **known**, and so on). Notice that the underline position below the baseline and the thickness of the underline are borrowed from the **FontInfo** dictionary in the current font, if it exists; if it does not, the values are hard-wired to **12** and **1**. This data actually exist (or should exist) upstream at the word processor.

NOTE: In Example 12.5 the underline thickness and position are *very* roughly calculated. In a real driver, these values should be much more carefully calculated based on the point size of the font being used and the recommended values provided in the font metrics files for the fonts. Rather than complicating this example unnecessarily, an overly simplistic algorithm was used to determine these values.

Let's look at two ways to eliminate some of the extraneous commands from this last example. The first is to pass down appropriate data for the underline position and thickness from the host, but continue to calculate the ending position in the PostScript driver. The other enhancement will be to introduce two slightly different versions of the **TEXT** procedure (one that underlines, one that doesn't) and set it up so that the **underlineON** and **underlineOFF** procedures select the right one. We'll also beef up the **underlineON** procedure to pass down the values for the position and thickness of the underline itself. Notice also the way that the **-ON** and **-OFF** procedures redefine the **TEXT** name to use the correct procedure (see Example 12.6).

Example 12.6: Simplifying the Underlining Code

```
/underlineON              % - underlineON -
{ %def
        /underline true def
        /underlinethick exch def
        /underlinebelow exch def
        /TEXT { TEXTwith } def
} def
/underlineOFF             % - underlineOFF -
{ %def
        /underline false def
        /TEXT { TEXTwithout } def
} def
/TEXTwithout { moveto show } bind def
/TEXTwith { %def
        moveto
        gsave
                0 underlineposition rmoveto
                underlinethickness setlinewidth
                dup stringwidth rlineto stroke
        grestore
        show
} bind def
```

```
/Times-Bold 24 selectfont
1.0 -5 underlineON
(Hamlet, Act II) 200 650 TEXT
underlineOFF

/Times-Roman 12 selectfont
(This should be the first line from Hamlet.) 72 600 TEXT
(And this, of course, the second.) 72 570 TEXT
```

The resulting program has a nice balance of data use, passing some of it from the host word processor, storing some of it, and reducing the complexity of the program itself in the way it relies on the data. Notice that the only change to the way we wanted to set the program up was to add two operands to the **underlineON** procedure call. The rest of it stayed the same.

CLASSICAL DATA STRUCTURES

There are some classic data structures in the field of computer science that you might want to construct in your PostScript program. For instance, you might want to make use of doubly-linked lists, queues, stacks, trees, and so forth. (Stacks are generally free in PostScript because of the inherent stack-based model, but sometimes you need to create your own.)

Linked Lists

Linked lists can be very useful data structures. A linked list is basically a sequential list of chunks of data that you can traverse either forward or backward (if it is doubly-linked). The main advantage to linked lists in traditional programming languages is that you can allocate memory as you need it, and it doesn't have to be contiguous. In each data block, you store a pointer to the next block, wherever it may be. In PostScript, the need for these lists diminishes greatly, since you don't need to worry about the way memory is allocated in order to access data. PostScript language arrays are arrays of other PostScript objects, each of which is self-contained (and very likely occupies some memory that is not adjacent to the next element in the array). But, readjusting the terminology very slightly, lists are still extremely useful, even if you don't have to spend much time worrying about the links between the elements.

Let's assume that you have a single block of data representing text from a drawing program. You want to store the *x*, *y* location of the text on the page, the font in which the text is to appear, the text itself, and the color. In the C language, you might come up with something like the code in Example 12.7.

Example 12.7: List Elements as C Structures

```
struct textchunk {
        float X,Y;                  /* X,Y location on screen */
        char font [ 128 ];          /* font name */
        float ptsize;               /* point size of font */
        float R,G,B;                /* color */
        char *text                  /* the text itself */
        struct textchunk *next;     /* link for list */
} *head, *tail;
```

What might be the best way to implement a composite data structure like a **struct** in PostScript? You have only a few choices.

- You could use an array that contains all of the pieces of data.
- You might use dictionaries, creating one for each chunk of data.
- You might simply accumulate piles of data on the operand stack, keeping track of what was where.

Since the operand stack is likely to be unwieldy for a structured approach such as this, let's consider arrays and dictionaries, to see which one seems better.

Using Arrays to Form Lists

Let's look at an array that contains everything that the C **struct** does, but which does not have the links to the next item in the list (see Example 12.8).

Example 12.8: List Elements as PostScript Array Objects

```
[
        72.0 100.0
        /Times-Italic
        24.0
        1.0 0.0 0.0
        (Julius Caesar)
]
```

Notice that the names have disappeared, since arrays contain just the data. But how would you create a link to the next chunk of data? Since a PostScript array object is already a pointer to a composite data structure, we could use it directly, including an array object within the array that represents the next item in the list. It looks as though the arrays are nested when you look at them syntactically, but in effect one array simply contains a pointer to another. An array might even contain a circular reference by including a copy of itself as one of its elements, but we will try to avoid that in our examples. Notice that the original array (the one containing the name *Julius Caesar*) has been reproduced, but is written a little more compactly to save some space on the page (Example 12.9).

Example 12.9: Forming a List of Array Objects

```
[
        72.0 650.0 /Times-BoldItalic 24.0 1 0 0
        (Julius Caesar)
        [
                72.0 600 /Times-Italic 18.0 1 0 0
                (William Shakespeare)
                []
        ]
]
```

The actual structure of these arrays looks more like Figure 12.1 when it is represented internally in the PostScript interpreter.

Figure 12.1: Structure of the PostScript Linked List

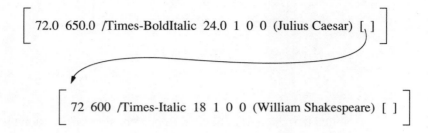

This method is very compact and efficient, but it does present one difficulty: the elements of the structure cannot be referred to by name, but only by their position within the array (although you could write procedures to help you with this). Arrays could be troublesome to maintain effectively and to debug, but are much more space-efficient than dictionaries.

Using Dictionaries to Form Lists

Let's try the same idea using a dictionary to store the elements of the structure (see Example 12.10).

Example 12.10: List Element as a PostScript Dictionary

```
/head 9 dict def
/tail head def
head begin
        /X 72 def
        /Y 470 def
        /font /Times-Roman def
        /ptsize 16 def
        % red, green, and blue stored as R,G,B:
        /R 1 def
        /G 0 def
        /B 0 def
        /text (Act One) def
        /next null def% points to nothing
end
```

When a new chunk of data is created to add to the list (in much the same manner as this one was created), the list may be maintained by judicious definition of the next name to point to the next chunk in the list (see Example 12.11).

Example 12.11: Linking a New Element to the List

```
9 dict begin
        % field definitions here
        /next null def        % end of list
currentdict end
dup head exch /next exch put
/tail exch def
```

Notice that the **next** pointer in the first chunk of data has been updated to be a reference to the newly-created list element, which is now stored as the **tail** of the list. The only elements in the list that have names are the **head** and **tail** entries in the list. The rest are anonymous, and can only be referenced by following the **next** pointers from the other dictionaries in the list.

Queues, Trees, and Other Data Structures

The concepts that have just been introduced for creating lists can easily be extended to create queues, stacks, or even trees of all sorts, since pointers are so easily created and assigned in PostScript.

For example, a queue can be implemented as a linked list of items that are always accessed in a first-in, first-out basis (FIFO). A stack could be built the same way, accessing the data on a last-in, first-out basis (LIFO), but it makes much more sense to use the PostScript operand stack to collect the objects if you need them in that order anyway. For more complicated structures like binary trees, you need only extend the basic "structure" model of a dictionary or an array to contain references to the appropriate elements of the tree. The structure of these classic data structures is beyond the scope of this book, but is discussed at great length in other volumes.

CONCLUDING THOUGHTS

Although the data structures we have discussed in this chapter are very sound principles in computer science, they may not be the most appropriate storage paradigm in your PostScript program. Think very carefully about the relationships between your data elements and the way that they will be created, used, and destroyed. Consider the benefits and drawbacks of arrays, dictionaries, and the operand stack before deciding on the final representation for your data structures. Keep these points in mind as you read about program data and instructions in the next chapter.

EXERCISES

1. When drawing a vertical line, you only need the x coordinate once, since it is the same for both endpoints of the line. Design a procedure called **V** that draws only vertical lines. Your procedure should be able to draw a line at any thickness, at any x,y location, and of any length.

2. In order to underline some text, you must determine the position and thickness to draw the line.

    a. What are the disadvantages to performing this calculation in your PostScript code?

    b. What are the disadvantages to performing the underlining calculation in your word processor application?

3. Create a data structure that could serve as a stack (you can restrict its size to 50 elements). Write two procedures called **stackpush** and **stackget** that will let you place objects on your stack and then retrieve them back again. The **stackpush** procedure should take just one argument—the object to be pushed onto the stack data structure. The **stackget** procedure should return one value onto the operand stack—the value retrieved from the stack data structure. Don't worry about stack overflow or underflow error conditions.

Chapter 13

Program Data and Instructions

Programs generally consist of instructions and data in the same sense that an arithmetic problem does: there are operations (such as addition or multiplication) and there are numbers or other data that are fed to those operations. However, in the same sense that you can't add without having a few numbers, many PostScript programs require data just to make them programs. Example 13.1 presents a very simple program to show the distinction between data and instructions in some typical code.

Example 13.1: Identifying Data and Instructions

```
/Times-Roman              % data
      findfont                    % instruction
24                        % data
      scalefont setfont           % instructions
100 300                   % data
      moveto                      % instruction
(Data and Instructions)   % data
      show                        % instruction
```

The dichotomy between the data and instructions in Example 13.1 can be made more clear by a slight rearrangement of the instructions into a procedure, which is then called with all of the data on the operand stack, as in Example 13.2.

Example 13.2: Separating Data and Instructions

```
/textset                    % (string) Xloc Yloc scale fontname textset -
{ %def
        findfont exch scalefont setfont
        moveto show
} bind def


(Data and Instructions) 100 300  24 /Times-Roman%data
textset                                     % instruction
```

But in another context, the font used and the position on the page might be part of the algorithm, and not really just data used by the algorithm. For instance, in a simple text formatter, the page number might always appear in a fixed location in a particular font, but the page number itself would be passed as data (see Example 13.3).

Example 13.3: Data as Part of the Algorithm

```
/pagenum                    % int pagenum -
{ %def
        306 36 moveto /Courier 12 selectfont
        (xxxx) cvs show
        showpage
} bind def

3               % data
pagenum         % instruction
```

A good working definition of data and instructions might be as follows: *instructions* are the fixed aspects of the program, and *data* are things that are provided by the user each time you run the program. That is a little more forgiving (and useful) than a very strict definition in which an operator (such as **moveto**) is always an instruction and its operands are always data.

But why does it matter? What advantage is there in making a distinction between the program's instructions and its data?

One of the most common sources of program bugs (having the wrong objects on the operand stack) can result when you change your mind about the interaction between a program and its data. For example, you might decide that the operands to your procedure should be presented in a slightly different order as an optimization, but you might forget to change one clause in your **ifelse** statement to reflect the change in data representation. There are other ways in which the distinction between data and instructions becomes important, as we see in the rest of this chapter.

TURNING DATA INTO INSTRUCTIONS

The instructions in your program are the fixed part, and the data are the elements that can be different each time you run the program. But there are circumstances in which data may actually be executed as instructions.

Let's look at an example. If you were to write an *emulator* in PostScript that made your printer pretend to be a line printer, then you may want to make it recognize some simple line printer commands among the lines of text to be printed. To simplify this somewhat, let's say that you want to recognize the *form feed* primitive that is often used in line printers. In particular, the ASCII character for form feed is octal 013. Example 13.4 is a very simple line printer emulator, written in PostScript, that will print any lines of text it gets, and will eject the page to start a new one whenever it encounters the form feed character. The form feed character has been changed to (X) instead of (\013) in this example so you can see the form feeds.

Example 13.4: Treating Carriage Return as an Instruction

```
% yet another line printer emulator
/left 36 def            % margins
/bottom 36 def
/top 792 48 sub def
/buffer 1024 string def
/setup                  % - setup -
{ %def
        /Courier 12 selectfont
        left top moveto
} bind def
/emulate                % - emulate -
{ %def
        { %loop
                currentfile buffer readline { %ifelse
                        (X) search { %ifelse
                                gsave show grestore
                                pop showpage setup
                        } if
                        gsave show grestore
                        0 -14 rmoveto
                        currentpoint exch pop bottom le { %if
                                showpage setup
                        } if
                }{ %else
                        showpage exit
                } ifelse
        } loop
} bind def
setup emulate
```

form feed is octal 013. Here is a very simple line printer emulator, written in
PostScript, that will print any lines of text it gets, and will eject the page to start a
new one whenever it encounters the form feed character:
Here comes a form feed X and some more text following it (should appear on the
new page).
X
Top of third page

There are many other possibilities for turning data into instructions.
Occasionally instructions must be read from a file rather than being
included in the program itself, in which case the instructions are data
while they are being read from the file, and before being executed.
Example 13.5 shows a simple looping program that reads lines from a file
and executes them (assuming that they are in fact PostScript instructions).

Although the **run** operator can perform precisely this task, the technique of looping through a file is still useful in many situations.

Example 13.5: Executing Data Found in a File

```
/datafile (/usr/local/lib/sample.ps) (r) file def
/buffer 1024 string def
{ %loop
      datafile buffer readline { %ifelse
              cvx exec       % execute the line of data just read
      }{ %else
              datafile closefile exit
      } ifelse
} bind loop
```

This simplistic program won't work with all data files, since it attempts to execute exactly one line of the program at a time. If any delimiters such as parentheses or braces are opened on one line but not closed until a subsequent line, the code will not execute correctly.

TURNING INSTRUCTIONS INTO DATA

A good example of turning program instructions into data is the task of *listing* (or printing out) a PostScript program so you can look at it on paper. You may have already run into this situation if you have worked much with the PostScript language. The previous example program that works as a simple line printer emulator actually does convert PostScript program code into data for typesetting if you should happen to feed it a file that contains PostScript. Example 13.6 shows this same emulator with slightly different data at the end. You might have to look closely to see that last ten lines of the program are not executed, but are printed on the page.

Figure 13.1 shows what the top of the output page would look like when the program in Example 13.6 is executed.

Example 13.6: Instructions as Data (to be Line Printed)

```
% even more line printer emulation
/left 36 def            % margins
/bottom 36 def
/top 792 48 sub def
/buffer 1024 string def
/setup                  % - setup -
{ %def
        /Courier 12 selectfont
        left top moveto
} bind def
/emulate                % - emulate -
{ %def
        { %loop
                currentfile buffer readline { %ifelse
                        (X) search { %ifelse
                                gsave show grestore
                                pop showpage setup
                        } if
                        gsave show grestore
                        0 -14 rmoveto
                        currentpoint exch pop bottom le { %if
                                showpage setup
                        } if
                }{ %else
                        showpage exit
                } ifelse
        } loop
} bind def
% everything after the following "setup emulate" line will be printed on
% paper instead of executed:
setup emulate
%!
/datafile (/usr/local/lib/sample.ps) (r) file def
/buffer 1024 string def
{ %loop
        datafile buffer readline { %ifelse
                cvx exec        % execute the line from the file
        }{ %else
                datafile closefile exit
        } ifelse
} bind loop
```

Figure 13.1: Output of Example 13.6

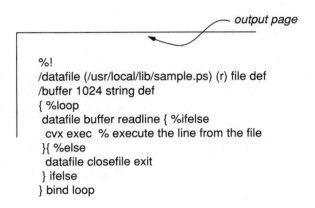

```
%!
/datafile (/usr/local/lib/sample.ps) (r) file def
/buffer 1024 string def
{ %loop
 datafile buffer readline { %ifelse
  cvx exec  % execute the line from the file
 }{ %else
  datafile closefile exit
 } ifelse
} bind loop
```

DATA CONVERSIONS

Quite a few PostScript operators convert one data type to another. Once you know that they exist, they are easy enough to use. There are also some fancy ways to accomplish data conversion in the next few sections. But first, some examples of common data conversions using the appropriate PostScript operators (see Example 13.7).

Example 13.7: Converting Strings to Numbers

```
(12456) cvi                         % 12456
(2898.87) cvi                       % 2899
(117.5) cvr                         % 117.5
(120) cvr                           % 120.0
(5837.9) cvx exec                   % 5837.9
(612.0) token pop exch pop          % 612.0
(612.0 792.0 moveto) token pop
exch token pop exch pop             % 612.0 792.0
```

Example 13.8 shows the conversion of decimal numbers to an octal or hexadecimal representation (the result is a string, since octal numbers do not exist in the interpreter except as notation).

Example 13.8: Converting Decimal Numbers to Octal or Hex

```
/scratch (0000) def
32 8 scratch cvrs                    % (40)
193 16 scratch cvrs                  % (C1)
(y) 0 get 16 scratch cvrs            % (79)
```

The program segments shown in Example 13.9 show how to convert back and forth between name and string data types, which are very similar in content. Remember that the slash (/) character often seen in programs is not really part of the name, but just the syntax used to express a literal name to the interpreter.

Example 13.9: Converting between Names and Strings

```
/scratch 128 string def
/Palatino-Roman scratch cvs          % (Palatino-Roman)
(Palatino-Roman) cvn                 % /Palatino-Roman
```

Example 13.10 shows one way to convert an array to a procedure. Since arrays are built in real time, you have to be careful not to accidentally execute something that you intend to be placed on the operand stack.

Example 13.10: Converting Arrays to Procedures

```
% careful about executable names:
[
        0 0 /moveto cvx
        /Optima 24.0 /selectfont cvx
        (Optima sample) /show cvx
] cvx
```

The **cvs** operator converts arbitrary data types to strings, which can be useful for printing out data. However, the **cvs** operator cannot convert composite objects like dictionaries or arrays to a string representation. An example of this simple kind of conversion is given in Example 13.11, with a workaround for composite objects. A better approach would be to use the **type** operator to explicitly determine the type of the object, then take some appropriate action to convert it to a string. Exercise 3 at the end of this chapter explores this concept more fully.

Example 13.11: Converting Arbitrary Data to Strings

```
% /scratch 128 string def
/printobject { %def
        dup 128 string cvs dup (--nostringval--) eq { %ifelse
                pop type 24 string cvs
        }{ %else
                exch pop
        } ifelse
} bind def
FontDirectory printobject
StandardEncoding printobject
```

CONCLUDING THOUGHTS

In this chapter, you've learned about data and instructions and how they can be converted from one to the other. You've also seen how various data types can be converted into other data types. These techniques will come in handy in the next chapter as you begin using files.

EXERCISES

1. Take the following code segment and rewrite it so that all the data are on the operand stack and all the instructions are inside a procedure. Since the example has two sets of data, please call your procedure twice, once with each set of data.

    ```
    100 200 moveto 0.5 setgray
    /Times-Roman findfont 96 scalefont setfont
    (G) show
    143 171 moveto 0.7 setgray
    /Times-Roman findfont 96 scalefont setfont
    (R) show
    ```

2. Write a procedure called **cvhex** that will turn an integer into a hexadecimal string and leave that string on the operand stack.

3. Write a procedure called **tabshow** that shows a string of text in the current font, but treats tab characters specially by moving the current point to the right by some fixed amount. (HINT: the ASCII code for a tab is 9.)

Chapter 14

Using Files and
Input/Output Techniques

Opening a file to read or write data is one of the most fundamental operations a program can perform. The PostScript language has good support for file operations, although some conceptual understanding of files is required to understand how to use these operators effectively.

File Objects

A file is always represented by a file object in a program. This is even true in other languages, such as C, where a file descriptor is used in all file references once you have opened the file. There is a *bona fide* PostScript object for file objects, and all of the file-related PostScript operators require the use of it. The **file** operator and the **currentfile** operator provide the two standard ways to obtain a file object.

Streams and Files

A *stream* is a special case of a file object that can only be accessed sequentially. You have no real way to know, given an arbitrary file object, whether or not you can read or write arbitrary parts of the file. It is best always to assume that the file is a stream, and only to read sequentially from it (or write sequentially to it). For example, the **currentfile** operator will often return the file stream representing the serial port on the printer, although it might represent a real disk file in an environment where there is a file system available to the interpreter. As long as you use the **setfileposition** operator with some care, the distinction between a stream and a file probably won't matter.

TIP Some file operations will work on virtually any PostScript interpreter, such as reading from the current file or writing to the standard output stream. Other file operations, such as explicitly opening a file by name, checking the status of a file, or using a very specific operator like **setfileposition**, depend heavily on the existence of a file system supported by the interpreter. It is very important to make sure that the interpreter supports these operations before attempting them, or you may get an error. You can use the **known** or **where** operators to check for the existence of certain operators, or you can consult the manual for your interpreter to find out how to test for the presence of a file system.

As a rule of thumb, any printer equipped with a hard disk or any workstation running a PostScript interpreter will have access to the full range of disk operations described in this chapter.

PostScript File Operators

Many PostScript operators read to, write from, or administer files. They differ quite a bit in the details, but they all work in pretty much the same way. Remember that you almost always need either a file object or a file name with each of these operators. Also, keep in mind that the reading and writing operators are analogous to the **get** and **put** operators. This will help you to conceptualize the file operations somewhat; they both require two basic pieces of information: what you want to read or write, and which file you are interested in.

Table 14.1 contains a list of PostScript file operators. Some of these operators are not available in early implementations of PostScript printers, especially those without hard disk capabilities.

Table 14.1: PostScript File Operators

Arguments	Operator	Action
string1 string2	**file** file_object	open file string1 with access string2
file_object	**closefile**	close file
string	**deletefile**[†]	remove file from device
string1 string2	**renamefile**[†]	change file name string1 to string2
pattern proc scratch	**filenameforall**[†]	execute proc for files that match pattern string (can use *)
file_object	**read** int true	read one character from file
	false	
file_object int	**write**	write one character to file
file_object string	**readhexstring**	read hexadecimal strings
	substring	
	boolean	
file_object string	**writehexstring**	write hexadecimal strings
file_object string	**readstring** string	read string from file
file_object string	**writestring**	write string to file
file_object string	**readline** string	read through newline
file_object	**token** token true	read PostScript token from file
	false	
file_object	**bytesavailable**[†] int	how many bytes left in file
	flush	flush stdout file
file_object	**flushfile**	flush file_object
file_object	**resetfile**[†]	reset file pointer to beginning of file
file_object int	**setfileposition**[†]	set file position to int
file_object	**fileposition**[†] int	return current position in file
file_object	**status**[†] boolean	is file_object still valid?
string	**status**[†] pages	return information on disk file named
	bytes	string and leave data on stack
	referenced	
	created	
	true	
	or	
	false	
	diskstatus[†]	
	pages_used	
	total_pages	
string	**run**	execute contents of file string
	currentfile file_object	returns currently active file object

string **print**	write string to *stdout* output file
any **=**	convert *any* to a string and write string to *stdout* file, followed by a newline
any₁.. anyₙ **stack**	print contents of stack
any **==**	convert *any* to a readable representation and write to *stdout* (works like =, but is more powerful), followed by a newline
any₁.. anyₙ **pstack**	print contents of stack non-destructively
prompt	used only in interactive (executive) mode
echo	used only in interactive (executive) mode

NOTE: Operators marked by a dagger are not available on all implementations (they are language extensions).

OPENING AND CLOSING FILES

To open a file in PostScript, you use the **file** operator (which you can think of as an "**open**" operator, for all practical purposes). Opening a file gives you a file object that you can then use for reading from or writing to that file. The only tricky part is to make sure that there really is a file to open.

The file operator requires a file name and a mode or permission string. The file name is obvious. The *mode* is how you specify that you want to open the file for reading, writing, or (in some implementations) appending. If you open a file for writing (not appending), it will instantly create a file of zero length, destroying any other file that might have existed with that name. Because of this you should be especially careful when you open files for writing the first few times.

Let's look at the syntax of the **file** operator a little more closely.

filename mode **file** *file_object*

The exact syntax of the **filename** operand depends, to some extent, on the environment in which the interpreter is running (see Table 14.2).

Table 14.2: Example File Names in Different Environments

Environment	Example File Name
UNIX	(/LocalLibrary/fonts/outline/Palatino-Roman)
Macintosh	**(:root:System Folder:PalatRom)**
DOS	(D:\FONTS\PALATROM.FNT)
PostScript	(fonts/Palatino-Roman)

You will have to find some documentation for your system that details the syntax for file names.

Table 14.3: Modes for Opening Files with *file* Operator

Mode	Explanation
(r)	open file for reading only
(w)	open file for writing and delete any existing contents of file

The best way to make sure that the file name you are about to use is valid is to use the **status** operator first (see Example 14.8 later in this chapter).

Example 14.1 shows some examples of the **file** operator in use, to give you the flavor of some file names and modes:

Example 14.1: Sample Use of the *file* Operator

```
% NOTE: this is not a working program, just several individual examples
% of using the file operator
(/etc/passwd) (r) file
(fonts/Palatino-Roman) (w) file
(%stderr) (w) file
(%stdin) (r) file
```

Once your file is open, you can read from it (if you opened it with a mode for reading) or write to it, as detailed in the next section. Don't forget to close it properly (with **closefile**) when you're done (Example 14.2).

Example 14.2: Closing a File

```
/file_object (/etc/passwd) (r) file def
% ...
file_object closefile
```

READING AND WRITING FILES

Once you have a valid file object, either from the **file** operator or the **currentfile** operator, you can read from it or write to it any number of times (or at least until you run out of data to read or until you fill up the file system).

The **read** operator (and its variants) returns an exit status boolean to let you know whether or not it succeeded. This lends itself nicely to an **ifelse** statement for error checking, unless you are very sure that the operation will succeed and you want the code to execute as fast as it can (which is, actually, fairly often the case).

Reading from a File

There are several PostScript operators that you can use to read from a file object. All but one require you to provide a buffer into which the operator can place the bytes read from the file. The exception is the **read** operator; it just reads a single byte from a file, and therefore it doesn't need a buffer. The size of the buffer is up to you. Most of the read operations in PostScript will simply read until they fill up your buffer. In contrast, the **readline** operator reads until it sees a specific end-of-line condition. This can create two possible error conditions.

1. You might run out of data to read before you fill your buffer.
2. You might run out of buffer space before you get to an end-of-line condition.

If you run out of data before the buffer is full, the operator you were using to read from the file will tell you (by leaving **false** on the stack). There is no general way to make sure that your use of **readline** won't overflow your buffer. If you're worried about it, you can certainly use a very large buffer (some implementations limit string sizes to about 64 kilobytes).

Example 14.4 illustrates use of the **readstring** operator to read data from a file and write it to a new file.

Writing to a File

Writing to a file is very similar to reading from a file, with a couple of exceptions. First of all, the writing operators do not return a boolean indicating their success or failure. And second, there are a few special character string conventions for such things as newlines and parentheses that apply to strings that you write to a file (detailed in Table 14.4).

Table 14.4: Special Characters

In String Body	Actual Character
\n	newline
\r	return character
\t	tab
\b	backspace
\f	form feed
\\	backslash
\(	left parenthesis
\)	right parenthesis
\XXX	three-digit octal character code, such as \037
\	a backslash followed by a newline indicates no character, and is used to continue a long line to avoid problems in environments where line lengths are restricted

The most common operator for writing to a file is the **writestring** operator, which takes an arbitrary string and writes it to the file object you supply. The string is written exactly, byte for byte, to the output file, with the exception of the special backslash escapes. In particular, **writestring** does not automatically add a newline or carriage return to each line of text written to the file. (If you want a newline, just put **\n** at the end of your string before you call **writestring**.)

The program in Example 14.3 writes the **StandardEncoding** array out to a temporary file.

Example 14.3: Writing an Array Out to a File

```
/tmpfile (/user/glenn/encoding.ps) (w) file def
/scratch 128 string def

tmpfile (/StandardEncoding [ \n) writestring
StandardEncoding { %forall
        tmpfile (    /) writestring
        tmpfile exch scratch cvs writestring
        tmpfile (\n) writestring
} forall
tmpfile (] def\n) writestring
tmpfile closefile
```

Copying and Renaming Files

In order to copy a file, you need to open it with mode (**r**), open the destination file with mode (**w**), and use the **loop** operator to read from one file and write to the other until you reach the end of the input file. Example 14.4 copies the file (**/etc/passwd**) to a new file named (**/etc/passwd.BAK**). It assumes that the original file already exists and can be opened for reading.

Remember to write out the last partial buffer. When the **readstring** operator returns **false**, there may be a few bytes in the substring that were read before the end-of-file indication was encountered. This can be seen in the **else** clause of the conditional in Example 14.4. The contents of the string are written before the files are closed and before the loop is finally exited.

Example 14.4: Copying a File

```
/infile (/etc/passwd) (r) file def            % open files and save file objects
/outfile (/etc/passwd.BAK) (w) file def
/buff 128 string def                          % your buffer for reading operations
{ % loop
        infile buff readstring { %ifelse
                outfile exch writestring
        }{ %else
                outfile exch writestring
                infile closefile
                outfile closefile
                exit     % exit the loop
        } ifelse
} bind loop
```

To rename a file, simply use the **renamefile** PostScript operator if it exists. The program in Example 14.5 checks for the existence of **renamefile** and if it is not found, it defines a procedure called **renamefile** that emulates the behavior of the operator by copying the file to the new name and then deleting the original file.

Example 14.5: Renaming a File

```
% emulate "renamefile" if it doesn't exist (copy the old file to the new and
% then try to delete the old file if possible)...
/renamefile where { pop }{ %ifelse
        /renamefile          % (oldname) (newname) renamefile -
        { %def
                (w) file /new exch def
                dup (r) file /old exch def
                /buff 256 string def
                { % loop
                        old buff readstring { %ifelse
                                new exch writestring
                        }{ %else
                                new exch writestring
                                old closefile new closefile exit
                        } ifelse
                } loop
                /deletefile where { pop deletefile } if
        } bind def
} ifelse
(/user/glenn/encoding.ps) (/user/glenn/StandardEncoding.ps) renamefile
```

WRITING FORMATTED DATA TO FILES

If you need to write out a data file or create a file with formatted data in it, you'll need to become very familiar with the whole family of file writing operators, as well as the data conversion operators (discussed in Chapter 13). Let's look at some useful techniques.

Writing Out Various Data Types

There are many different PostScript data types. Some of them are easy to write to a file; others present some challenges. To overgeneralize, simple data types (including integer, real, boolean, and mark) are relatively easy to convert into strings and write to a file, whereas composite objects such as dictionaries and arrays require some extra steps.

Let's look at a few procedures that will help you write out some data types to a file. Example 14.6 and Example 14.7 provide some code that you can draw from. The basic idea is to turn your data into a string, then write that string to the output file with the **writestring** operator. Example 14.6

---

shows you how to write numbers and names to a file. You should be careful about white space and newline characters to keep the syntax of the numbers and names correct.

Example 14.6: Writing Numbers and Names to a File

```
/fd (outputfile.ps) (w) file def
/scratch 1024 string def


/Wnum                        % num Wnum -
{ %def
        scratch cvs fd exch writestring
} bind def
/Wname                       % /name Wname -
{ %def
        dup type /nametype ne { %ifelse
                fd (% invalid name\n) writestring pop
        }{ %else
                dup xcheck not { fd (/) writestring } if
                scratch cvs fd exch writestring
        } ifelse
} bind def

FontDirectory { %forall
        pop Wname
        fd (\n) writestring
} forall

fd closefile
```

Notice that the **Wnum** procedure in Example 14.6 doesn't pay much attention to the type of its operand, so you could use it for either an integer or a real number. The beauty of the **cvs** operator (used inside the **Wnum** procedure to convert the number to a string) is that it is polymorphic; it doesn't matter what type of object you present to it, as long as there is a reasonable string equivalent. The **Wname** procedure is very much the same as the **Wnum** procedure, except that it prints a leading slash if the name presented to it is a literal name. Note that the slash is not part of the name itself. The slash syntax helps you to create a literal name when your program is parsed for the first time, but it just sets the literal flag on the name object, and does not otherwise differ from an executable name.

Spaces, Tabs, Returns, and Special Characters

If you intend to do any serious formatting of the output file, you will need to create white space, and you may need to write out some special characters. For the most part, the backslash syntax used for special characters will do this for you (see Table 14.4). To get them into your output file, just put them into a string body and write that string to the file with the **writestring** operator. You may find it convenient to use some procedures to do this for you, such as those found in Example 14.7.

Example 14.7: White Space and Special Characters

```
/fd (outputfile.ps) (w) file def
/scratch 1024 string def

% these procedures all depend on "fd" being a valid output file descriptor
/Wname                      % /name Wname -
{ %def
        dup type /nametype ne { %ifelse
                fd (% invalid name\n) writestring pop
        }{ %else
                dup xcheck not { fd (/) writestring } if
                scratch cvs fd exch writestring
        } ifelse
} bind def
/Wstring { fd exch writestring } bind def
/Wline                      % (string) Wline -
{ %def
        fd exch writestring return
} bind def
/space                      % - space -
{ %def
        fd ( ) writestring
} bind def
/return                     % - return -
{ %def
        fd (\n) writestring
} bind def
/tab                        % - tab -
{ %def
        fd (\t) writestring
} bind def
```

```
% the following three lines of code will reproduce the
% first two lines of this program in the output file:
(%!) Wline
/fd Wname space ((outputfile.ps) (w) ) Wstring
/file cvx Wname space /def cvx Wname return

fd closefile
```

FILE STATUS INFORMATION

One of the most useful bits of information about a file is the number of
bytes it contains. On most PostScript interpreters with file systems
(including printers with a hard disk), there are two ways to determine this.
The first is the **status** operator, to which you pass a file name. The **status**
operator actually provides several kinds of information about the file,
including how many *pages* of disk space it occupies (a page is typically
1,024 bytes), when it was last accessed, when it was written, and how
many bytes it contains. Here is the syntax of the **status** operator.

filename_string **status**

> *pages bytes referenced created true*

or

> *false*

The **status** operator returns a boolean which is **false** if the file exists, **true**
otherwise. If the file exists, the **status** operator also returns the other fields
shown in the syntax of the **status** operator. Example 14.8 shows the
status operator in use.

Example 14.8: Using *status* to Check a File

```
% this code opens a file for reading if it exists, else error message
(/etc/passwd) dup status { %ifelse
        4 { pop } repeat       % get rid of interesting file data
        (r) open
}{ %else
        print ( is not a valid file name. Cannot open.\n) print flush
        stop
} ifelse
```

NOTE: The **status** operator and the **bytesavailable** operator may not be present in all implementations of the PostScript language. It is wise to check for its existence before using it.

If the file is already open and you have a file object that represents it, you can use the **bytesavailable** operator to determine how many bytes remain in the file object. If you have already read some of the bytes, **bytesavailable** will always return the remainder, or 0 if there are no more bytes to be read.

Here is the syntax of the **bytesavailable** operator:

file_object **bytesavailable** *int*   how many bytes left in file

The program in Example 14.9 uses the **bytesavailable** operator to pick a random number for file access.

NOTE: The **bytesavailable and setfileposition** operators may not be present in all implementations of the PostScript language. It is wise to check for its existence before using it.

Example 14.9: Random File Access with *setfileposition*

```
% get a random word from UNIX dictionary file:
/fd (/usr/dict/words) (r) file def          % open the file
rand fd bytesavailable mod                   % random number within file size
fd exch setfileposition                      % seek to that position in the file
fd 128 string readline pop pop               % read partial line (at random position)
fd 128 string readline pop                   % read entire line --> your word
100 600 moveto
/Times-Italic 24 selectfont show
```

RANDOM VERSUS SEQUENTIAL ACCESS

Under normal circumstances, you should treat a file as though it were only readable sequentially. That way, your program will not break if it is transported into another environment where files may be implemented differently. If you really need to perform random access on a file object, the **setfileposition** operator will help you. You need to open the file either for read (**r**) or write (**w**) to use the **setfileposition** operator (see Example 14.9).

If you try to set the file pointer beyond the end of the file with **setfileposition**, you will get an **ioerror**, so be careful that you know how big the file is (using either the **status** or the **bytesavailable** operator).

CONCLUDING THOUGHTS

This chapter presented a broad overview of file operations in PostScript and how to use them effectively. PostScript supports file I/O operations in much the same way that other languages do, assuming that you have an interpreter with full support for a file system. Remember, these and other language extensions must be used somewhat carefully to make your code truly portable across all implementations of the PostScript interpreter.

You should now have a pretty solid understanding of the PostScript language and how it relates to other languages that you already know. Hopefully by now you have even started to enjoy the fact that PostScript works backwards and upside down, and you have learned to appreciate its strengths and unique language characteristics—in short, you have learned how to think in PostScript.

The simplicity and power of PostScript makes it a very good language to write programs quickly and confidently that work the very first time, like many of the examples in this book. By now you will have developed a strong programming style and technique that lets you rough out a program, look up the syntax of an occasional PostScript operator, and proceed quickly with the knowledge that you are doing the right thing—and in one of the world's most interesting programming languages.

EXERCISES

1. Write a procedure that finds all the fonts on the local hard disk specified as **(fonts/FontName)** and write just the font names to the standard output file. (HINT: use the **filenameforall** operator.)

2. Adapt the program from Exercise 1 to write both the font names and the byte sizes of the font files to the standard output file.

3. Write a program that will open a file called **prog.ps** and execute the file one token at a time (using the **token** and **exec** operators), writing

each token to another file called **trace.ps**. This program might be useful for debugging **prog.ps**, since you can determine exactly how much of the file **prog.ps** has been executed by looking in the trace file. Don't worry about getting the tokens to look exactly right in the output file, as long as something gets written for each one and the program executes to completion without error. (HINT: You will need to be very careful with procedure bodies.)

4. In Exercise 2, you may have noticed that a lot of PostScript language tokens do not have readable representations once they have been tokenized by the interpreter. Expand on Exercise 2, making sure that strings, procedure bodies, and literal names are represented correctly in the output file. You should be able to actually execute the resulting **trace.ps** file and get the same results as the original file.

Appendix

Appendix

Answers to Exercises

CHAPTER 1

1. Your answers to the question *Why do you want to write a PostScript program?* will be varied, and there is no answer to this exercise, of course. Here are some potential responses that might stimulate some thought.

- You want to write a driver to control a laser printer.
- You are writing a graphics application for a computer system that uses PostScript for display graphics.
- You want to modify the behavior of an existing PostScript program, or to add functionality to (or fix bugs in) an existing piece of application software you have been using.
- You want to include graphics in a text document you are preparing.
- You are interested in PostScript as a programming language, and want to write any program you can.
- You want to write fractal programs to draw fancy pictures on your display or on your printer.

These answers may seem contrived, but consider that the program you write to include a figure in a paper you are writing may be dramatically different than a graphics application running on a PostScript display and even more different than a laser printer driver.

2. PostScript is a "backwards" (post-fix) language in order to minimize the overhead, and to permit a program to be executed directly from a stream or file without fitting the whole thing into memory.

3. PostScript is an interpreted language in order to keep it device independent and to make it more portable. It also allows a program to be executed directly from a file, regardless how long or complicated the program is.

4. It is silly to write fractal programs in PostScript because the calculations necessary to draw fractals usually are complex and take forever in an interpreted language like PostScript. Also, since the pictures themselves are generally static (the same picture will be drawn each time you execute the program), it makes more sense to execute the fractal algorithm in a compiled language, and generate a PostScript description of the resulting image. That is a use of the PostScript language that is more in keeping with its design.

CHAPTER 2

1. Notice that no variables or names are required to implement this factorial algorithm. There are, of course, many other ways to accomplish this task.

```
1    % leave on stack
10 -1 0 { mul } for
(10 factorial is ) print ==
```

2. Here are some possibilities for PostScript's greatest strengths as a programming language.

   • It is extensible and flexible.
   • It is standard, extremely portable, and machine-independent.
   • It is an interpreted language, making it easy to debug.
   • It has many powerful "convenience" operators.

Here are some candidates for its greatest weaknesses.

- It is an interpreted language, making it fairly slow.
- It is not highly structured.
- It does not interface easily with other compiled languages.

3. Here are several language constructs that are available in both the C and PostScript languages, of which you may have come up with four. There may be others, as well.

- **while** loops
- **if** statements
- the ability to define and call procedures
- built-in mathematical operations for addition, subtraction, multiplication, division, exponentiation, etc.
- boolean operations for **and**, **not**, **or**, and related bit-wise operations
- array and string data types.

4. Here are some capabilities of the PostScript language that are not available in other languages (you may have come up with any three from this list, or perhaps others).

- built-in typographic operators for typesetting text (the **show** operator or the **findfont** operator, for example)
- the *dictionary* data type
- the *name* data type
- the "path and paint" graphics model for constructing shapes and filling or stroking them with color
- device-independent halftoning for shades of gray or color
- the ability to convert literal data types into executable program fragments (for example, you can create an array of objects and then make it an executable procedure body with one instruction).

CHAPTER 3

1. The only syntax errors you can get arise from mismatched delimiters.

a) The parentheses are not nested correctly. The interpreter will read past the (part 1) looking for the closing parenthesis. The corrected code should be either of the following.

```
0 1 20 { ( Hello world (part 1)) == flush } for
0 1 20 { ( Hello world \(part 1) == flush } for
```

b) The syntax error in this program is the incorrect nesting of { } brackets in the **ifelse** statement. The first clause does not have a closing bracket. Better indentation shows this problem much more clearly.

```
currentpoint exch 32 gt { %ifelse
        72 lt { %if
                showpage 36 500 moveto
        } if
{ %else
        (hello world \(part 2) show
} ifelse
```

missing }

2. Here is a simple procedure named **line** that takes four operands, the *x, y* location for the beginning of the line and the *x, y* location for the end of the line.

```
/line                    % X1 Y1 X2 Y2 line -
{ %def
    4 -2 roll moveto
    lineto stroke
} bind def
100 150 300 600 line
650 75 50 500 line
```

3. Here is a template for a procedure that contains an **ifelse** statement.

```
/myproc                 % - myproc -
{ %def
    A B gt { %ifelse
          % if A is greater than B
    }{ %else
          % B is greater than A
    } ifelse
} bind def
```

4. Here is a procedure called ++ that will increment a variable.

```
/++               % /anyname ++ -
{ %def
    dup load      % load current value onto stack
    1 add         % add 1 to that value
    def           % store it back into same name
} bind def
/counter 0 def
/counter ++
/counter ++
counter ==        % should be 2
```

CHAPTER 4

1. In a page description, the prologue of procedure definitions should be made as readable as possible, but the script that is generated by the application should be made compact and efficient, since the prologue is only executed once per document, but each procedure may be called many times in the script.

2. Here are the kinds of PostScript programs that you might expect to consume memory.

- downloaded font programs
- programs that load procedures into memory
- documents with string data in the body
- any program that stores data.

3. There is no reasonable way to use query programs in an environment with one-way or batch communications.

CHAPTER 5

1. The **stringwidth** operator returns a value for both x and y, a fact that is often overlooked. The value **0** is left on the operand stack, since only the y value is consumed from the call to **stringwidth**.

2. Here are the errors found in the various program segments.

   a. This code segment raises no errors.

   b. There is a **typecheck** error on command **scalefont**. Remember that the **findfont** operator returns a dictionary on the operand stack that is used by **scalefont**, but the scale factor is in the wrong position on the stack. This could be fixed simply by changing **scalefont** to **exch scalefont** in the exercise.

   c. There is a **typecheck** error on command **show**. The trick in this exercise is to remember that **stringwidth** returns two values, one for y and one for x. The 0 y component is used inadvertently instead of the value for x, resulting in **0 0 rmoveto**, then the x value is on the stack when **show** is called, resulting in **typecheck**.

   d. There is a **typecheck** error on command **restore**. Remember that the **restore** operator leaves an object on the operand stack, and this object is required by **restore**. In the exercise, the string body is duplicated with **dup** before **show**, leaving a copy on the stack when **restore** executes. If you came up with **invalidrestore**, you were close. If the code had been **exch restore** instead of just **restore**, an **invalidrestore** error would have occurred, since the string object that was still on the stack was created more recently than the last **save**, making it illegal to **restore** as long as an instance of the string is still on the operand stack. To fix this, you would need **pop restore** instead of **restore**, or simply to remove the **dup**.

3. This is a fairly difficult problem. Once you eliminate the local dictionary and the **exch def** lines, you have to start thinking carefully about what is on the stack, where it is, and exactly how many times you will need it. Here is one answer.

```
36 750 moveto /Times-Roman 24 selectfont
% works like "show", leaving current point at proper location
/ushow                    % linethick lineposition (string) ushow -
{ %def
    gsave
         exch 0 exch rmoveto
         dup stringwidth rlineto
         exch setlinewidth stroke
    grestore
    show
} bind def
0.5 -4 (test underlined text) ushow
```

The following figure shows the output of this code.

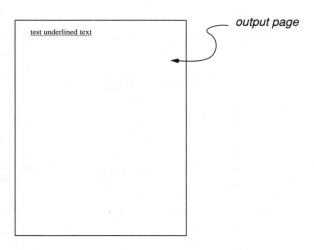

CHAPTER 6

1. Each time around the **for** loop, the loop index is pushed onto the operand stack and is added to the number that is already on the stack (which starts out as **0**). The program is equivalent to the following arithmetic expression.

   0 + 10 + 20 + 30 + 40 + 50 + 60 + 70 + 80 + 90 + 100

   The result of this expression (and of the exercise) is 550.

2. Here is the program segment again. The results left on the operand stack after its execution follow.

   ```
   clear
   /A /B /C /D /E /a /b /c /d /e
   2 copy 6 index 6 index 12 -4 roll exch 5 3 roll

   % results on operand stack.
   /A /B /b /c /d /e /d /e /a /D /a /E /b
   ```

3. This is a pretty tricky task. Here is a procedure called **reversestack** that will reverse the contents of the operand stack (the topmost element becomes the bottom element). Notice the clever use of the **for** operator and the loop variable it provides. Notice also that the loop begins at **2** to avoid a **1 -1 roll**.

   ```
   /reversestack          % any_0 ... any_n reversestack any_n ... any_0
   { %def
       2 1 count 2 sub { %for
           % use the loop counter as argument to "roll"
           -1 roll
       } for
   } bind def
   /a /b /c /d /e /f /g reversestack
   ```

4. Here is a procedure called **standardfonts** that finds all fonts defined in **FontDirectory** that have a standard encoding. This procedure leaves the names of the fonts on the operand stack.

```
/standardfonts          % - standardfonts font_0 ... font_n
{ %def
    FontDirectory { %forall
        /Encoding get StandardEncoding ne { pop } if
    } forall
} bind def

standardfonts
```

CHAPTER 7

1. Here is a sample program that implements a **case** operator. It is certainly not the best nor the only way to implement it. Compare this version to the one you came up with.

```
/case                   % mark proc bool_0 proc_0 ... bool_n proc_n case -
{ %def
    % requires a pair of operands on
    % the stack for each option: the
    % matching case item and a procedure.
    % You must have a mark at the bottom
    % of your case pairs, and you must
    % supply the thing to be tested on
    % the top of the operand stack:
    % mark { default }
    % case3 { proc3 }
    % case2 { proc2 }
    % case1 { proc1 }
    % item_to_test case
```

```
        /test_item exch def% save this
        exch dup type /marktype ne { %ifelse
            test_item eq { %ifelse
                    counttomark 2 add 1 roll
                    cleartomark
                    exec
            }{ %else
                    pop
            } ifelse
        } %else
            exec   % default case
        } ifelse
} bind def
```

2. The following procedure installs an emulation of the **setcmykcolor** language extension by using the **where** operator to define this procedure *only* if the **setcmykcolor** operator does not already exist.

```
/setcmykcolor where { %ifelse
    pop          % don't need the dictionary
}{ %else
    /setcmykcolor { %def
        1 sub 4 1 roll
        3 { %repeat
                3 index add neg dup 0 lt {pop 0} if 3 1 roll
        } repeat setrgbcolor pop
    } bind def
} ifelse
```

3. Here is a rewrite of the **image** procedure body to check for the end-of-file condition reported by the **readhexstring** operator.

```
/picstr 16 string def
100 100 translate 100 900 scale
16 2 8 [ 16 0 0 16 0 0 ]
{ %image
    currentfile picstr
    readhexstring not { %if
        (ERROR end of file) == flush
        stop
    } if
} bind image
00FF00FF00FF00FF00FF00FF00FF00FF
00FF00FF00FF00FF
```

CHAPTER 8

1. The loop index is used directly as provided by the **for** operator on the operand stack. Notice that neither the loop index nor the factorial variable are stored into a dictionary. They are used directly from the operand stack.

```
1    % leave 1 on stack
10 -1 1 { mul } for
(10 factorial is ) print ==
```

2. The only trick to this is to rearrange the data in the opposite order on the operand stack and to provide the correct number for the loop constraint.

```
0 0 moveto
600 600
500 600
400 400
300 400
200 200
100 200
6 { lineto } repeat closepath fill
```

3. Notice the way the loop in the following segment of code takes advantage of the way the **search** operator works, and uses the arguments in a very natural way.

```
(Here is a string with some spaces in it)
/count 0 def
dup                % save the original string body
( )                % a space
{ %loop
    search { %ifelse
        pop /count count 1 add store
    }{ %else
        pop exit
    } ifelse
} bind loop
```

4. Remember that the **forall** operator, when applied to a string body, leaves the integer byte value of each character on the operand stack. A string comparison won't work, so we need to compare it to the byte value for a space (retrieved directly from a string to maintain device-independence).

```
(Here is a string with some spaces in it)
dup                % save the string
0                  % initial value of counter
( ) 0 get          % byte code for space
3 -1 roll          % 0 32 (Here is a string...)
{ %forall
    1 index eq { exch 1 add exch } if
} bind forall
pop                % byte code for space
                   % counter is now on top of stack
                   % original string is just below it
```

5. There were two bugs in the program, each of which alone would result in a **typecheck** error on **restore** when executing the program. In both cases, the problem was that the loop index was left on the operand stack. In the first loop, the **dup** operator should not have been used, since it caused the loop index to be left on the stack after each iteration. In the second loop, the **1 index** had the same effect, and should have been simply **exch**.

```
% draw a grid of 20 x 10 lines
save
    0.1 setlinewidth
    20 20 translate
    0 10 200 { %for
        % dup
        0 moveto 0 100 rlineto
    } for
    stroke
    0 10 100 { %for
        % 0 1 index moveto 200 0 rlineto
        0 exch moveto 200 0 rlineto
    } for
    stroke
restore
```

CHAPTER 9

1. The secret is to rearrange the order in which the data are provided on the operand stack to suit the order in which the operators in the procedure require data.

```
/TEXT                    % (string) ptsize /fontname X Y TEXT -
{ %def
    moveto
    findfont exch scalefont setfont
    show
} bind def
(This is an example of Times-Bold)
24 /Times-Bold 100 100 TEXT
```

2. This requires copying one of the procedures.

```
/concatprocs            % proc₁ proc₂ concatprocs proc₃
{ %def
    dup length 2 add array
    exch 1 index 2 exch putinterval
    dup 1 /exec cvx put
    dup 3 1 roll 0 exch put
    cvx
} bind def
```

Here is another alternative that uses a LOCAL dictionary.

```
/concatprocs              % proc₁ proc₂ concatprocs proc₃
{ %def
    LOCAL begin
        /proc2 exch def
        /proc1 exch def
        /new /proc2 load length 2 add array def
        new 2 /proc2 load putinterval
        new 1 /exec cvx put
        new 0 /proc1 load put
        /new load cvx
    end
} bind def
/concatprocs load 0 3 dict put
```

3. Here is a procedure called **def** that is functionally equivalent to the built-in **def** operator. The key is to use the **put** operator, and to make sure the entry goes into the current dictionary.

```
/def                      % key value def -
{ %def
    currentdict 3 1 roll put
} bind def
```

4. Here is a "debugging" version of the **moveto** operator. Make sure you don't get into a recursive loop; **load** the existing value of **moveto** into your procedure.

```
/moveto load
/moveto                    % X Y moveto -
{ %def
    LOCAL begin
        dup /Y exch def
        1 index /X exch def
        X 612 gt Y 792 gt
        X 0 lt Y 0 lt or or or { %if
                (errant X: ) print X ==
                (errant Y: ) print Y ==
        } if
    end
    MOVETO
} bind def
% replace LOCAL (in position 0 of proc):
/moveto load 0 2 dict put
% replace MOVETO (in last position of proc):
/moveto load dup length 1 sub 3 -1 roll put
```

CHAPTER 10

1. The value left on the operand stack after executing the following short program segments is **16**. The following walk-through of the program segment shows how that answer was derived.

```
/variable 7 def        % define /variable in current dict
5 dict dup begin       % new dict on op-stack and dict-stack
    /variable 9 def    % /variable is 9 in new dict (both places)
end                    % remove one copy of new dict from dict-stack
/variable dup load     % loads from original (current) dict => 7
3 1 roll get           % "get" from new dict copy still on op-stack (9)
add                    % 7 + 9 = 16
```

2. The following definition for **boxproc** replaces the dictionary named **LOCALDICT** with an anonymous dictionary.

```
/boxproc                % X Y W H boxproc -
{ %def
    REPLACE_ME begin
        /height exch def
        /width exch def
        /Y exch def
        /X exch def
        X Y moveto
        0 height rlineto
        width 0 rlineto
        0 height neg rlineto
        closepath
        fill
    end
} %now replace the dictionary
dup 0 12 dict put bind def
```

3. These three operators in the PostScript language have an effect on the dictionary stack: b**egin**, **end**, **currentdict**.

4. This program shows the names of all fonts stored in **FontDirectory**.

```
FontDirectory { pop == } forall
```

CHAPTER 11

1. The contents of the array constructed by the code

```
[ 0 0 moveto 100 100 lineto currentpoint ]
```

are simply [100 100]. The code in between [and] is actually executed, and only the final **currentpoint** operator leaves anything on the operand stack.

2. Here is some PostScript code to create a two-dimensional array 5 elements wide and 10 elements deep.

```
[ 5 { 10 array } repeat ]
```

Another, more straightforward way to get this would be

```
[ 10 array 10 array 10 array 10 array 10 array ]
```

This actually produces a single array with 5 arrays as its elements; each sub-array contains ten elements. Although this can be thought of as a two-dimensional array, there is actually no easy way to access an element in two-space. You have to use the get operator twice, once on the primary array, and again in the sub-array.

3. Here is a procedure called **extractfontname** that will take a string like **(fonts/Palatino-Roman)** as input and strip off the **(fonts/)** part of the name, leaving just **(Palatino-Roman)**.

```
/extractfontname      % (fonts/FontName) extractfontname (FontName)
{ %def
    dup length 6 sub 6 exch getinterval
} bind def
(fonts/Palatino-Roman) extractfontname
```

CHAPTER 12

1. To create a procedure that draws a vertical line, you will need to get some data from somewhere, but you can generate some of the data internally within the procedure. In particular, you only need the x location of one of the endpoints, and need not duplicate that data. Here is a procedure called **V** that does this.

```
/V                          % linewidth Height Xloc Yloc V
{ %def
    gsave
            moveto              % Xloc and Yloc from stack
            0 exch rlineto      % use Height from stack
            setlinewidth        % use linewidth from stack
            stroke
    grestore
} bind def

3.5 150 200 200 V
1.0 125 300 200 V
```

2. The calculation of where to put the underline and how thick to make it depends on several things. First of all, the position of the underline depends on the text being underlined—both its position on the page and its point size (the underline should be further away from the text baseline for larger text). This font information is available in the PostScript interpreter as well as in Font Metric files or other tables in the host environment.

    a. The main disadvantage of performing this calculation in your PostScript program is performance; it will take some time to execute in PostScript. Also, it will increase the complexity of your PostScript code a fair amount. The other disadvantage is that you don't know anything else about the page on which you're underlining text. For example, if you underline three words in a row, each of which is in a different font, you would prefer not to have the underline change thickness beneath the second or third word, and there is no reasonable way to know about this at the PostScript level.

---

b. The main disadvantage of doing underline calculations in your word processor is that you may not have the font metric information available to you on the host end, or the information could be mismatched with the actual font used in the interpreter.

3. An array turns out to be the most convenient data type to use to implement a stack. You will need a variable that serves as a stack pointer (to point to the top of the stack) and two procedures, **stackpush** and **stackget**. The following code implements all of this.

```
/STACK 50 array def        % the stack data structure
/PTR 0 def                 % the stack pointer

/stackpush                 % any stackpush
{ %def
    STACK exch PTR exch put
    /PTR PTR 1 add def
} bind def

/stackget                  % stackget any
{ %def
    /PTR PTR 1 sub def
    STACK PTR get
} bind def

(Testing) stackpush
/Times-Roman 24 stackpush stackpush
72 600 stackpush stackpush

stackget stackget moveto
stackget stackget selectfont
stackget show
```

CHAPTER 13

1. Here are the two sets of data separated from the instructions.

```
/myproc                 % (string) /FontName ptsize gray Xloc Yloc myproc
{ %def
    moveto setgray
    exch findfont exch scalefont setfont
    show
} bind def

(G) /Times-Roman 96 0.5 100 200 myproc
(R) /Times-Roman 96 0.7 143 171 myproc
```

2. Here is a procedure called **cvhex** that takes an integer and turns it into a hexadecimal string. It just uses the **cvrs** operator.

```
/scratch 128 string def
/cvhex                 % int cvhex <hex_string>
{
    16 scratch cvrs
} bind def

1245 cvhex
```

3. Here is a procedure called **tabshow** that shows a string of characters, moving 24 points to the right for each tab character encountered.

```
/tabshow                % (string) tabshow
{ %def
    { %loop
        (\t) search { %ifelse
                show            % show pre string
                pop             % get rid of tab
                24 0 rmoveto    % move current point
        } { %else
                show exit
        } ifelse
    } loop
} bind def

/Times-Roman findfont 24 scalefont setfont
100 100 moveto (abc\tdef\tghi) tabshow
```

CHAPTER 14

1. Here is a program that will write all the font names from the hard disk to the standard output file.

```
(fonts/*) { %filenameforall
    dup length 6 sub 6 exch getinterval
    print (\n) print flush
} 128 string filenameforall
```

2. Here is an adaptation of Exercise 1 that includes the byte sizes of the font files, too.

```
(fonts/*) { %filenameforall
    dup dup length 6 sub 6 exch getinterval
    print ( ) print
    status { %if
        % status returns: pages bytes referenced created
        pop pop exch pop (XXXXXXX) cvs print
    } if
    (\n) print flush
} 128 string filenameforall
```

3. Here is a program that will open a file called **prog.ps** and execute the file one token at a time, writing each token to an output file.

```
% open prog.ps and execute one token at a time, writing each token
% to trace.ps as you go

/infile (prog.ps) (r) file def
/outfile (trace.ps) (w) file def
/buff 65535 string def          % very large buffer
```

```
{ %loop
    infile token { %ifelse
        dup buff cvs
        outfile exch writestring
        outfile (\n) writestring
        dup type /arraytype ne { %if
            exec                    % execute the token
        } if
    } { %else
        infile closefile
        outfile closefile
        exit
    } ifelse
} bind loop
```

4. Here is the program from Exercise 2, enhanced to handle procedures, arrays, and names correctly in the output file.

```
/infile (prog.ps) (r) file def
/outfile (trace.ps) (w) file def
/buff 65535 string def          % very large buffer
/writeout                  % (string) writeout
{ %def
    outfile exch writestring outfile (\n) writestring
} bind def
/writeany       % any writeany
{ %def
    dup type /arraytype ne { %ifelse
        dup type /nametype eq { %ifelse
            dup xcheck not { outfile (/) writestring } if
            buff cvs writeout
        }{ %else
            dup type /stringtype eq {
                outfile (\() writestring
                outfile exch writestring
                (\)) writeout
            }{ %else
                buff cvs writeout
            } ifelse
        } ifelse
    }{ %else
```

```
        dup xcheck { %ifelse
                ({ %begin procedure) writeout
                        { outfile (    ) writestring writeany } forall
                (} %end procedure) writeout
        }{ %else
                % can't have any other kind of array
                (% encountered regular array) writeout
        } ifelse
    } ifelse
} bind def

% loop through the input file, reading and executing
% the tokens
{ %loop
    infile token { %ifelse
        dup writeany
        dup type /arraytype ne { exec } if
    } { %else
        infile closefile
        outfile closefile
        exit
    } ifelse
} bind loop
```

Indexes

Index of
Example Programs

Chapter 8: Using Looping Constructs 93

Chapter 9: Procedures 105

Chapter 13: Program Data and Instructions 157

Chapter 14: Using Files and Input/Output Techniques 167

Subject Index

A
algorithms 6, 12, 158
allocating memory 29
argument passing 76
arithmetic 27
array object 51
arrays 135
    concatenating 139
    construction 135
    converting to procedures 164
    for linked lists 152
    versus dictionaries 141
ASCII 2

B
backslash 20
backspace 173
basic skills 17
begin 22
begin operator 126
booleans 82
braces 20, 22
bytesavailable operator 169, 179

C
C programming language 9

C structures 152
carriage return 160, 173, 177
case statement 79
closefile operator 31, 169
closing a file 170
comments 20
comparison of objects 32
composite objects 30, 51, 61
concatenating arrays 139
concatenating strings 139
conditionals 73, 79
    compound 88
    constructing 80
    nesting 87
    templates for 80
    true and false 81
currentfile operator 167, 168, 169, 172
cvs operator 164

D
data
    converting types 163
    storing and using 145
    versus instructions 157
data on operand stack 69
data storage in dictionaries 119

data structures 6, 69, 141, 151, 155
data types 51
def operator 54, 126
definitions 21
deletefile operator 169
delimiters 20
dictfull error 123
dictionaries 119
    for linked lists 154
    global 123
    local 121
    versus arrays 141
dictionary stack 62, 63, 75
disk (*see* files) 167
diskstatus operator 178
displays 4
Document Structuring Conventions 21
dup operator 71

E

emulator, line printer 159, 161
Encapsulated PostScript 43
end operator 126
EPSF 43
equality 32
error, syntax 19
/etc/passwd 174
example programs 37
exch def 61, 70
exch operator 71
executable names 60
execution model 54
execution stack 62, 63
exitserver operator 46

F

file objects 167
file operator 167, 169
filenameforall operator 169

files
    copying and renaming 174
    file naming 171
    open modes 171
    opening and closing 31, 167, 170
    random access 179
    reading and writing 168
    reading instructions from 160
    sequential access 179
findfont operator 57
flow charts 12
font names 98
font programs 40
for loops 93
forall operator 127
form feed 159
functions 76, 105

G

get operator 126
goto 3
graphics state stack 62, 63
grouping 56

H

hard disk (*see* files) 167
hard disk status 178

I

ifelse operator (*see also* conditionals) 79
image operator 100
immediate name lookup 29
indentation 20, 22
index operator 71
input/output 14
instructions versus data 157
intuition 56
ioerror 180

K

known operator 129

L

language
  // notation 28
  arrays versus dictionaries 141
  dictionaries 119
  extensibility 13
  indentation 22
  name lookup 53
  name scoping 120
  names 26
  syntax 19
  thinking backward 58
last-in, first-out 60
line printer 161
linked lists 151
local dictionaries 121
local variables 76
loop operator 174
loops 73, 93
  as procedure bodies 99
  exiting 102
  finding font names 98
  image operator 100
  loop index 95
  table of arguments 98
  table of operators 94
  template for 94
  using **bind** 99

M

memory 29

N

name lookup 29, 53, 60
name scoping 120
names 26, 60
  converting to strings 164
  writing to a file 176
naming conventions 111, 113
naming procedures 111
newline 173

O

numbers
  converting from strings 163
  converting to octal or hex 163
  writing to a file 176

object types 32
objects
  composite 51, 61
  converting to strings for printing 164, 175
  simple 51
octal characters 173
opening a file 170
operand stack 53, 56, 67, 146
operands 60
operators, redefining 130

P

page description 37
parameter passing 108
parentheses 20
persistently resident programs 46
postfix 58
prefix 58
preview 45
procedures 105
  arguments 59
  concatenating 114
  constructing good 111
  converting to arrays 164
  defining 21, 107
  efficiency 111
  interleaving data 109
  naming 111
  organization 111
  overview 106
  parameter passing 108
  perspective on 11
  self-modifying 114
program development cycle 17
program structure 20

programming cycle 18
prologue 21
pstack operator 170
put operator 126

Q

query programs 43
queues 155

R

read operator 169
readhexstring operator 82, 169
reading data 42
reading data from a file 142
readline operator 169, 172
readstring operator 172, 174
recursion 76
redefining operators 130
renamefile operator 169, 174
repetitive algorithms 5
roll operator 71, 72
run operator 161, 169

S

save object 51
search path 13
self-modifying procedures 114
setfileposition operator 168, 169, 179
shared memory 47
showpage operator 131
simple object 51
software cycle 19
stack
    dictionary 62
    looping 73
    overview 53
    rearranging 71
    rolling 72
    trusting the 67
StandardEncoding 173
status operator 169, 178
stream (*see* file) 168

string object 51
strings 135
    concatenating 139
    construction 137
    converting to names 164
    converting to numbers 163
    I/O 140
    put and **get** 137
    scanner syntax 137
structured programming 3
style
    ifelse statements 24
    indentation 22
    local dictionaries 121
    naming conventions 113
    templates 24
syntax 19
    // name lookup 28

T

tab character 173, 177
templates 24
token operator 169
transfer function 114
trees 155
trusting the stack 67
type operator 127
typecheck operator 75
types 32
typical programs 37

U

underlining 147
UNIX 13
UNIX files 171, 179
/usr/dict/words 179

V

variables 22, 26, 146
visual chunking 56

W

where operator 75, 129
while loops 93
while operator 79
window systems 4
write operator 169
writestring operator 169, 173

> $22.95 FPT US
> $29.95 CANADA

Thinking in PostScript®
Glenn C. Reid

LEARN THE ART OF POSTSCRIPT PROGRAMMING FROM AN EXPERT!

PostScript®, the dynamic page description language from Adobe Systems, Inc., has become an industry standard. It is incorporated into many of the most powerful printers and computers available today. Glenn C. Reid, the acclaimed author of Adobe's *PostScript Language Program Design*, now brings his expertise to **Thinking in PostScript,** an essential guide for every PostScript programmer from the novice to the advanced developer.

Thinking in PostScript begins with a concise overview of the PostScript language. The book then helps programmers build a solid foundation for understanding PostScript by showing how to combine elements of the language into a streamlined program. Advanced programmers will learn sophisticated techniques for making their programs more efficient and effective. The book also provides numerous practical examples in all areas of PostScript language programming, including the Display PostScript® system and other implementations. In this volume you will also find:

- never-before-published information on the PostScript language
- useful algorithms for loops, conditionals, and I/O
- detailed coverage of files, strings, and dictionaries
- simple and elegant programming techniques

Such detailed coverage from a recognized PostScript expert enables readers to learn how to perform every kind of PostScript programming task and makes **Thinking in PostScript** the ideal resource for all PostScript programmers.

Glenn C. Reid is the well-known author of Adobe's *PostScript Language Program Design* (Addison-Wesley, 1988). In addition, he worked at Adobe Systems, Inc., for four and a half years as a programmer and Manager of Technical Support to PostScript software developers. He most recently worked as the Product Manager of Interpersonal Computing at NeXT, Inc., one of the foremost advocates of the Display PostScript system. Glenn currently is a consultant and software developer in the UNIX® and Display PostScript marketplace.

Cover design by Doliber Skeffington

The text of this book is printed on 100% recycled paper.

Addison-Wesley Publishing Company, Inc.

5229

ISBN 0-201-52372-8

52372